AMSTERDAM
Like a Local

BY THE PEOPLE WHO CALL IT HOME

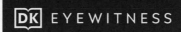

AMSTERDAM
Like a Local

BY THE PEOPLE WHO CALL IT HOME

Contents

NIGHTLIFE

OUTDOORS

meet the locals

ELYSIA BRENNER
After growing up in the US, Elysia landed in Amsterdam in 2006. Here she lives the freelance lifestyle, combining writing with exploring Amsterdam's streets and canals.

NELLIE HUANG
Singapore-born travel writer Nellie has lived in Miami, London and Spain, but it's Amsterdam she calls home these days. When she's not on the road, you'll find her kayaking down canals or barbecuing with friends.

MICHAL MORDECHAY
Michal has called Amsterdam her home since 2015, trading the Tel Aviv heat for the fickle Dutch weather. Outside her work, she loves biking, hunting for sunny swimming spots and going to live music gigs.

ROXANNE WEIJER
Back in 2012, Roxanne moved to Amsterdam from a small town nearby to study, and she never left (though she is partial to travelling the world). In her spare time, you'll find her playing sports and trying new food.

Amsterdam

WELCOME TO THE CITY

Expats lured by tech start-ups, families seeking a fresh beginning, students living their best lives: Amsterdammers make up a real patchwork of people. And that's nothing new. This city, shaped for centuries by immigration, has long been a beacon for the independent-spirited, where differences aren't just tolerated but are, in fact, celebrated. The locals here may appear a little abrasive but under that direct exterior, Amsterdammers look after one another, whether fighting for the first legally recognized gay wedding, championing the rights of sex workers or ensuring cyclists rule the road.

The city is as varied as its people – a hybrid of history and forward-thinking, exuberant energy and convivial charm, buzzing capital and laid-back small town. History is woven into every brick and beam, with gabled mansions lining the scenic canals, Rembrandt masterpieces ruling the galleries and

cosy *gezellig* bars little changed for decades. And yet while the city is passionate about preserving the past, locals aren't set on sitting still. Derelict shipyards have been transformed into restaurants and techno nightclubs, while cutting-edge design takes over new galleries.

With so many glorious contradictions, it can be hard to know where to start. That's where this book comes in. We know the places locals love best, from the live music bars that foster new talent to the brown pubs where folks linger till late. Of course, these pages can't capture the experience of every Amsterdammer, but instead offer a snapshot of this wonderful city.

So, whether you're a long-time local uncovering the unknown or a visitor wanting to rip up the traditional to-do list, this book will help you embrace the many sides of this multicultural city. Enjoy Amsterdam, the local way.

Liked by the locals

"Living in Amsterdam reminds you life's meant to be enjoyed. It has all the amenities of a city ten times its size, but everything is more accessible. And all that water!"

ELYSIA BRENNER, WRITER, EDITOR, TRANSLATOR
AND WINE PROFESSIONAL

*From spring blooms and festivals to **gezellig** (super-cosy) winter gatherings and saunas, there's a cause for celebration with each new season in Amsterdam.*

Amsterdam
THROUGH THE YEAR

SPRING

FESTIVAL FUN
As Amsterdam emerges from winter, festival season begins. Locals flock to Westerpark, Amsterdamse Bos and NDSM, to name but a few places, for food, music and theatre celebrations that carry on through to the autumn.

KONINGSDAG
On 27 April the Netherlands celebrates the king's birthday (King's Day). Crowds dressed in orange gather for huge flea markets and street parties in the capital.

TULIP SEASON
Come April, locals have one thing on their mind: to see the tulip fields near Lisse. Heading out of the city on their bikes, they skip the tourist-filled Keukenhof Gardens, cycling a little further north alongside the fields near Hillegom.

AJAX FOOTBALL
You can catch Amsterdam football club Ajax in play most of the year, but spring pairs good weather with watching the exciting last fixtures of the football season.

SUMMER

ON THE WATER
Whether they're dipping in the city's lakes, lounging on Zandvoort beach or sailing along the canals, the locals know the water's the place to be when the mercury soars.

PRIDE

Come early August, crowds take to the streets with rainbow flags while brightly festooned boats cruise the canals, with upbeat music pumping out of portable speakers. Why? It's Pride, of course.

OUTDOOR CINEMAS

While the nights are long and balmy, open-air cinemas spring up across the city. A favourite is the Pluk de Nacht festival in August when deck-chair-reclining film-lovers watch arthouse flicks on the Stenen Hoofd.

AUTUMN

THEATRE

As the autumnal chill sets in, theatre-lovers cosy up in big venues and tiny pop-ups for quirky plays during the Amsterdam Fringe Festival. Podium Mozaïek draws those who love stories to its International Storytelling Festival.

ELECTRONIC DANCE PARTIES

The biggest international club festival in the world, October's epic Amsterdam Dance Event sees party-goers boogie-ing all day and night to electronic beats in the city's clubs and parks.

MUSEUM NIGHT

For one night on the first weekend of November, Amsterdam's cultural hotspots throw open their doors until 2am for cool workshops, live music and extended exhibitions.

WINTER

FESTIVE LIGHTS

Light displays mark the start of the festive season. Families and friends cycle the city, admiring illuminated bridges and gawking at projections covering iconic buildings.

ICE-SKATING

Winter isn't winter without ice-skating. If the canals don't freeze over, everyone skates on the outdoor artificial rinks around Amsterdam – Jaap Eden IJsbaan and Museumplein are go-tos.

SAUNAS

In the coldest months, steaming in saunas at the city's many spas is a local ritual. For an added festive treat, folks soak in the out-door hot tubs on the roof of the Volkshotel, complete with skyline views and live music.

There's an art to being an Amsterdammer, from the do's and don'ts of canal cruising to negotiating the city's cycle paths. Here's a breakdown of the essentials.

Amsterdam
KNOW-HOW

For a directory of health and safety resources, safe spaces, and accessibility information, turn to page 186. For everything else, read on.

EAT
Breakfast and lunch are usually light, quick affairs, with the main meal of the day savoured at dinner. Fair warning: the Dutch are early eaters, with many kitchens closing by 11pm (though some stay open until later on Fridays and Saturdays). It's best to book a table for an early start if you want to linger over your meal as the locals do.

DRINK
Don't confuse coffee houses with coffeeshops. The former are integral to city life – locals are caffeine-addicts, after all. The latter serve soft drinks and cannabis. Looking to smoke? Strictly speaking, you need to be a Dutch citizen to buy cannabis, but many coffeeshops don't check this. Some in the city would rather tourists stayed away from coffeeshops, so do your research, heed local advice and if you're new to cannabis, take it slow.

Borreltijd (after-work drinks) starts around 5pm – any earlier, and locals will usually raise an eyebrow (unless it's at brunch). If you're planning a boozy picnic, only drink in the city parks: Pride and King's Day aside, drinking on the street could earn you a hefty fine.

SHOP
Amsterdam gets off to a sleepy start when it comes to shopping – especially on Mondays, when some stores might not open until noon. Most operate from 9am to 6pm on other days of the week, with supermarkets staying open until

10pm and *nachtwinkels* (night shops) selling pricey basics until 1 or 2am.

ARTS & CULTURE

The major museums are 9–5 affairs, though smaller galleries often stay open later. The big names don't come cheap, so it may be worth investing in a Museum or City Card if you're visiting multiple places. Definitely book online if possible: it will save you hours of queuing. Evening entertainment comes at all price points (even free) and the scene is pretty casual.

NIGHTLIFE

Nights out usually start with pre-drinks in a bar. At 1 or 2am, the party moves to nightclubs and after-hours bars, which stay open until 3 or 5am (a few even keep going 24-hours at the weekend). Some clubs have tough door policies, so check out the vibes and dress to match. Locals usually tip the bouncer on the way out. The drinking age is 18; if you look under 30, carry ID. Remember that this is a city where people live, so don't be too loud after hours (you may get fined) and refrain from overindulging.

OUTDOORS

When the sun's out, Amsterdammers flock to occupy every slice of outdoor space – it's even a legit reason to leave work early. Check your chosen park's regulations for things like barbecues and take any rubbish with you.

Boaters beware: sound and speed regulations are strict in city canals, and your skipper *will* be breathalyzed.

Keep in mind

Here are some more tips and tidbits that will help you fit in like a local.

» **Card vs cash** While the *pinpas*, or debit card, rules in Amsterdam (with only some credit cards accepted), it's always worth having some cash with you.

» **Smoking** Smoking tobacco inside (even in coffeeshops) is a big no-no. If you have to light up, do so outside in a designated area.

» **Tipping** A tip of around 10 per cent is the norm in restaurants. In taxis and bars, round up to the nearest euro.

» **Stay hydrated** Amsterdam is home to lots of water fountains, so bring a reusable bottle.

GETTING AROUND

Amsterdam is split into seven boroughs – Centrum (Centre), Noord (North), Oost (East), Zuid (South), West, Nieuw-West (New West), and Zuidoost (Southeast) – plus firmly attached "independent" towns like Amstelveen and Diemen. Each borough is like a Russian nesting doll of historical neighbourhoods; Borneoeiland, for example, is found in the Eastern Docklands, which is part of the larger Zeeburg neighbourhood, itself part of Oost. Confused? Don't worry: even Amsterdammers don't know the names of the most localized 'hoods on the other side of town.

To make your life easier we've provided what3words addresses for each sight in this book, meaning you can quickly pinpoint exactly where you're heading with ease.

On foot

Walking is your best bet for getting around Amsterdam's crowded city centre, where nothing's more than 20 minutes away by foot. The rest of the city is equally walkable, if you have the time and endurance (it'd take a few hours to cross the whole town). The locals are surprisingly leisurely strollers, so you won't feel hurried. Just learn quickly to identify bike paths (tip: look for pink pavement) and keep an eye out for tram rails, being careful to steer well clear of both. And if you do need to stop and check your phone or a what3words location, step to the side.

On wheels

You don't need us to tell you that cycling is the main mode of transport in Amsterdam. The experience can be chaotic, so a bike tour is a good way to learn the ropes. Ride only on dedicated cycle lanes *(fietspaden)*, which have their own traffic lights and road signs.

Amsterdam doesn't have a city bikeshare scheme but there are plenty of rental outfits to choose from; some, such as MacBike, offer optional extras like panniers and rain gear. Get a demo of the locks and make sure you use them: bike theft is rife. Locals notably forgo protective gear when cycling, spoilt by laws that breed cautious car drivers, but this is the only time we'll advise you not to do as the locals do: always wear a helmet. Another absolute essential is lights; those who don't use them after dark face a €90 fine.

Bikes are free on ferries but cost a few extra euros on dedicated train and metro carriages (outside rush hour). Sadly, they aren't welcome on trams or buses. *www.macbike.nl*

By public transport

Gemeente Vervoerbedrijf (GVB) runs Amsterdam's transport network, which handily links up with Schiphol Airport, the NS and Eurostar train networks, and various other cross-country services. Using the system is easy; you just need to pick up an OV-chipkaart (a contactless smart card). These come in two forms: a one-time-use card for either one hour or one to seven days, or a reloadable pass; both can be used across the tram, bus and metro networks. Most ferries are free, while trains require separate paper tickets, unless you're using a reloadable OV-chipkaart (for which you need a minimum balance of €20).

By car and taxi

Amsterdam doesn't want to be a car-friendly city; the plan is to eventually make the centre a car sharing-only zone where people rent cars for short periods of time. Narrow streets, canals, parking shortages and complicated one-way systems make getting around by car difficult so it's only worth driving if you really must. For the same reasons, taxis can be slow and expensive. If you do want a cab, use the Taxicentrale Amsterdam (TCA) app, the ubiquitous Uber or the cheaper ViaVan.

Download these

We recommend you download these apps to help you get about the city.

WHAT3WORDS

Your geocoding friend

A what3words address is a simple way to communicate any precise location on earth, using just three words. ///inhales.perform.watching, for example, is the code for beloved brown pub Café de Druif. Simply download the free what3words app, type a what3words address into the search bar, and you'll know exactly where to go.

9292

Your local transport advice

For the most accurate travel information you should turn to 9292. The app covers all modes of transport – trams, buses, ferries and trains – day and night, in Amsterdam and beyond.

Amsterdam is a patchwork of village-like mini-neighbourhoods, each with its own personality. Here we take a look at some of our favourites.

Amsterdam
NEIGHBOURHOODS

Bos en Lommer & De Baarsjes

Built in the mid-1900s, these conjoined 'hoods with a strong Muslim community saw a wave of urban renewal and influx of cool dining spots in the 1990s. Now, they're the place to be. *{map 2}*

De Pijp

Students, young creatives and a large LGBTQ+ community live in thriving De Pijp. After all, it has everything they want: hip bars, cafés and a distinct lack of tourists. *{map 3}*

Grachtengordel

Concentric rings of canals, lined with old, leaning buildings: this is quintessential Amsterdam. Few can afford to live here, but locals still pop by for museum mooching. *{map 2}*

Indische Buurt

One of the city's most multicultural areas, this has seen traditional halal shops replaced by slick bars in the 2000s. It's managed to hold onto its lively, culturally diverse vibe, though, with time-honoured restaurants standing strong. *{map 4}*

Jordaan

Massive gentrification has driven rent prices up in this neighbourhood but its narrow streets still have an offbeat feel, lined with open-air markets, cosy bars and quirky shops. *{map 2}*

NDSM

The city's most famous hipster industrial zone is growing up. Alternative arty spots have made way for commercial sites, drawing the media crowd, but the area is still awash with edgy street art. *{map 5}*

Nieuw-West

Cheaper rents and vibrant restaurants are making this the place to put down roots. But despite its trendy vibe it remains down to earth, thanks to the Sloterplas lake and park and the Meervaart community theatre. *{map 6}*

Nieuwendam

Time seems to have stood still in this former fishing village, where pretty houses sit beside courtyards. No surprise, then, that it's a big hit with families and bike-riding locals seeking some quiet time. {map 6}

Nieuwendamm-erham

Not to be confused with the similarly named village to its north, Nieuwendammerham is picking up the mantle from NDSM as the industrial cool kid. It's full of garages-turned-bars and hubs for sports like bouldering and skate-boarding. {map 6}

Oude Centrum

Old Amsterdam vibes live on in this part of town, full of centuries-old buildings and cosy brown pubs. Its canal-and-cobblestone charms are undeniable, but so are the high-season crowds (to the chagrin of locals). {map 1}

Oud-Oost

The old streets surrounding the Oosterpark are changing fast, with cool bars and shops springing up. Add to that a burgeoning festivals scene and folks have no reason to leave. {map 4}

Oud-West

Ever since the Foodhallen opened in 2005, Oud-West has been one of the city's top food quarters. These days, cool restaurants continue to draw foodies in their droves. {map 2}

Oud-Zuid

It's only the wealthiest Amsterdammers who live in this area, full of huge mansions, fancy restaurants and boutiques. But everyone can look (and dream) wistfully while they visit the world-class Stedelijk Museum, Concertgebouw and Rijksmuseum. {map 3}

Plantagebuurt

Though the city's former Jewish district was devastated during World War II, Plantagebuurt has found a new lease of life today. It's a revitalized green oasis, where young families come to visit the leafy parks and gardens. {map 4}

Westerpark

When Amsterdammers want a change of scene from the city's busy streets

they head to Westerpark. Its namesake park isn't the only thing it has to shout about: think old industrial buildings housing endless cafés and restaurants (with terraces), and more festivals than anywhere else in town. {map 2}

Zeeburg

Almost everything in the Oostelijk Havengebied (Eastern Docklands) was built in the last few decades (even many of the islands themselves), filling this area with striking, large homes that tempt young professionals to move in. Exciting architecture aside, hip bars, restaurants and swimming spots keep residents busy. {map 4}

Zuidoost

A 40-minute bike ride from town, this multicultural suburb with a big Surinamese community has seen its once-drab 1960s tower blocks made over into attractive, inexpensive housing. This, coupled with eclectic restaurants, lures students and young Amsterdammers to this lively spot. {map 6}

Amsterdam

ON THE MAP

Whether you're looking for your new favourite spot or want to check out what each part of Amsterdam has to offer, our maps – along with handy map references throughout the book – have you covered.

KOOG
AAN D
ZAAM

Noordzeekanaal

WESTPORT

S102

N200

ZWANENBURG

HAARLEM

N205

A9

A5

N232

SCHALKWIJK

OSDORP

HEEMSTEDE

N205

BADHOEVEDORP

A9

N208

N201

A4

N232

OVERBOS

A5

Amsterdam
Airport
Schiphol

HOOFDDORP

N205

N201

N232

A4

AALSMEER

N201

0 kilometres   3
0 miles   3

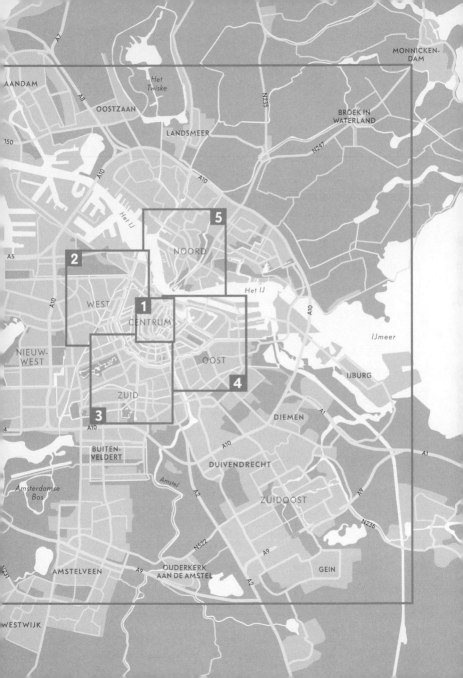

Gebroeders
Niemeijer **E**

Bitterzoet **N**

STATIONS-PLEIN

Open

Havenfron

HEKELVELD

In Aep **D**

Proeflokaal de
Ooievaar **D**

Tales & Spirits **D**

**NIEUWE
ZIJDE**

Tony's Chocolonely
Superstore **S**

Brouwerij de
Prael **D**

D Prik

S United Nude

Cut Throat
Barber & Coffee **E**

Red Light Secrets:
Museum of Prostitution **A**

Henk Comic
& Manga Stor

E Breda

CENTRUM

Koninklijk
Paleis

DAM

Black Heritage and
Colonial History Tour **A**

S De Bierkoning

PIJLSTEEG

De Bekeerde
Suster **D**

Nieuwma

DAMSTR.

Wok to Walk **N**

The Hash,
Marijuana and
Hemp Museum **A**

S Happy
Bookieman

FuLu
Mandarijn **E**

Bubbles &
Wines **D**

N The Jam
Society

De Brakke
Grond **A**

Bis!

S Locals

A Frascati

**OUDE
CENTRUM**

D Bierfabriek

S The Book
Exchange

Lanskroon
Bakery

Athenaeum
Boekhandel

E

S

S American
Book Center

E

Pannenkoekenhuis
Upstairs

Boekhandel
Perdu **S**

SPUI

S De Boekenmarkt
op het Spui

A Allard Pierson
Museum

S Droog

N Cannibale
Royale

Frens
Haringhandel **E**

S Scheltema

Mulligans Irish
Music Bar **N**

Amstel

AMSTEL

0 metres 200
0 yards 200

MAP 1

1

Gelderskade

E Lastage

Café 't
Mandje

KROMME

GELDERSEKADE

WAAL

Hemelse **E**
Modder

E
Los Pilones

NIEUW-
MARKT

BOOMSLOOT

KROM

OUDESCHANS

Oudeschans

JODENBREESTRAAT

JODENBUURT

WATERLOO-
PLEIN

WATERLOOPLEIN

Brediusbad

**SPAARNDAMMER-
BUURT**

TASMANSTRAAT

Museum
Het Schip

SPAARNDAMMERSTR.

WESTERPARK

Westerpark to
Nieuwe Meer Bike Ride

Het
Ketelhuis

Westergas
Sunday Market Radio Radio

Westerpark

Tonton Club West

Brouwerij Troost

De Bakkerswinkel

Haarlemmervaart

HAARLEMMERWEG

HAARLEMME
PLEIN

**STAATSLIEDEN-
BUURT**

VAN HALLSTRAAT

Singelgracht

Th
Movie

Checkpoint
Charlie

EERSTE MARNIX-
PLANTSOEN

**BOS EN
LOMMER**

ADMIRAAL

Podium
Mozaïek

KAREL DE RUIJTERWEG

DOORMANSTRAAT

Back to Black

FREDERIK
HENDRIK
PLANTSOEN

NASSAUKADE

Moooi Amsterdam
Brand Store

WESTER-
STRAAT

Café de Tuin

JORDAAN

JAN VAN GALENSTRAAT

KOSTVERLORENVAART

FREDERIK HENDRIKSTRAAT

Electric Ladyland

LGBTQ
History To

Erasmuspark

GALENSTRAAT

JAN VAN

Ram's Roti

Harar
Coffee

De Nieuwe Anita

WESTER-
MARKT

Grillroom
Shoarma Mesut

Salmuera

Bonboo

DE BAARSJES

Café Soundgarden

Boom
Chicago

Café de
Laurierboo

WEST

JAN EVERTSENSTRAAT

WITTE DE WITHSTRAAT

Kauffmann

Moak Pancakes

DE CLERCQSTR.

Singelgracht

Maloe
Melo

ELANDSGRACHT

PRINSENGRACHT

ADMIRALENGRACHT

2 Klaveren

Old West

Fabus

Meatless
District

Waterkant

KWAKERS-
PLEIN

LIJNBAANSGRACHT

OUD-WEST

LOT61 Coffee
Roasters

Kevin Bacon Bar

KOSTVERLORENVAART

Ten Katemarkt

KINKERSTRAAT

Seoul Food

The Maker
Store

NASSAUKADE

We are
Vintage

Jacob van Lennepkanaal

MAP 2

Oude Houthaven

2

Westerdok

GROTE BICKERSSTR.

HAARLEMMER HOUTTUINEN

Brouwersgr.

Prinsengracht

Keizersgracht

Singel

D Vesper Bar

D Het Papeneiland

S Noordermarkt

O Those Dam Boat Guys

D Proeflokaal Arendsnest

A Embassy of the Free Mind

D Rederij Paping

CENTRUM

RACHTEN-GORDEL

S Laura Dols

S Zipper

A Grachtenmuseum

Herengracht

Keizersgracht

🄴 EAT

🄳 DRINK

🅂 SHOP

🄰 ARTS & CULTURE

🄽 NIGHTLIFE

🄾 OUTDOORS

WEST

KINKERSTRAAT

NICOLAAS BEETSSTRAAT

BILDERDIJKSTR.

NASSAUKADE

Lijnbaansgracht

Prinsengracht

CENTRUM

Vegan Junk Food Bar **N**

Pathé Tuschins **E**

Duke of Tokyo **N**

Club NYX **N**

A

Eatmosfere **E**

A LAB111

E TEDS **S**

Little Plant Pantry

OVERTOOM-BUURT

Hap-Hmm **E**

Umaimon **E** **N**

The Waterhole **N**

N Melkweg **E** **N** **E** New York Pizza

Internationaal Theater Amsterdam

The Cave **N**

Rock Club **N**

Casa del Gusto **S**

Kattenkabinet

A

FOAM
Photography Museum

LEIDSE-PLEIN

Café Alto **N**

Jazz

Maxim Pianobar **N**

BAR-becue CASTELL **N**

Shiraz **D**

Paradiso **N**

WETERINGSCHANS

VIJZELSTRAAT

Prinsengrach

Lijnbaansgracht

Gollem's Proeflokaal **D**

OVERTOOM

VAN BAERLESTRAAT

STADHOUDERSKADE

E Lalibela

N OT301

Vondelpark

Vondelpark to Amsterdamsebos Bike Ride **O**

Rijksmuseum **A**

Boerenwetering

Singelgracht

MOCO Museum **A**

MUSEUM-PLEIN

E De Waaghals

Albert Cuypmark **E**

S Albert Heijn

MUSEUM-KWARTIER

Royal Concertgebouw

WILLEMSPARKWEG

JACOB OBRECHTSTRAAT

Warung Spang Makandra **E**

Burger Bar **N**

S

Lillie Wine Rebel **D**

OUD-ZUID

GOVERT FLINCKSTRAAT

HOBBEMAKADE

Scandinavian Embassy **D**

DE LAIRESSESTRAAT

ROELOF HARTSTRAAT

Coffee & Coconuts **D**

Glou Glou **D**

Omelegg **E**

Toomler **N**

Noorder

Amstelkanaal

ZUID

FERDINAND BOLSTR.

iambe **N**

DE PIJP

APOLLOLAAN

Yamazato **E**

O Boaty

Atelier Munro **S**

GERRIT VAN DER VEENSTRAAT

BEETHOVENSTRAAT

CHURCHILL - LAAN

MASSTRAAT

APOLLOBUURT

STADIONWEG

E Le Fournil de Sébastien

A Queen's English Theatre Company

DIEPENBROCKSTRAAT

PARNASSUSWEG

Zuider Amstelkanaal

Beatrixpark

SCHELDEBUURT

EUROPA-PLEIN

0 metres 500

0 yards 500

MAP 3

 EAT

De Waaghals *(p50)*

Eatmosfera *(p47)*

Golden Temple *(p50)*

Hap-Hmm *(p42)*

iambe *(p39)*

Lalibela *(p44)*

Le Fournil de Sébastien *(p37)*

Little Collins *(p34)*

Omelegg *(p34)*

STACH *(p39)*

TEDS *(p32)*

Umaimon *(p44)*

Vegan Junk Food Bar *(p48)*

Warung Spang Makandra *(p43)*

Yamazato *(p52)*

D DRINK

Coffee & Coconuts *(p83)*

Glou Glou *(p72)*

Gollem's Proeflokaal *(p67)*

Lillie Wine Rebel *(p73)*

Rayleigh & Ramsay *(p74)*

Scandinavian Embassy *(p81)*

Shiraz *(p72)*

S SHOP

Albert Cuypmarkt *(p88)*

Albert Heijn *(p98)*

Atelier Munro *(p94)*

Casa del Gusto *(p99)*

Little Plant Pantry *(p96)*

Veloretti *(p92)*

A ARTS & CULTURE

FOAM Photography Museum *(p116)*

Internationaal Theater Amsterdam *(p122)*

Kattenkabinet *(p129)*

LAB111 *(p125)*

MOCO Museum *(p119)*

Pathé Tuschinski *(p127)*

Queen's English Theatre Company *(p123)*

Rijksmuseum *(p117)*

Royal Concertgebouw *(p120)*

N NIGHTLIFE

BAR-becue CASTELL *(p157)*

Burger Bar *(p158)*

The Cave Rock Club *(p143)*

Club NYX *(p138)*

De Kleine Komedie *(p147)*

Duke of Tokyo *(p153)*

Jazz Café Alto *(p141)*

Maxim Pianobar *(p140)*

Melkweg *(p151)*

New York Pizza *(p159)*

OT301 *(p138)*

Paradiso *(p148)*

Pata Negra *(p157)*

Toomler *(p146)*

The Waterhole *(p143)*

O OUTDOORS

Boaty *(p176)*

Vondelpark *(p164)*

Vondelpark to Amsterdamsebos Bike Ride *(p170)*

N Bimhuis

E Mediamatic   **O** Rederij Lampedusa

D Hannekes Boom

PIET HEINKADE

Dijksgracht

N Mezrab

N Panam

OOSTERDOKSKADE

Oosterdok

PRINS HENDRIKKADE

OUDE WAAL

Oudeschans

Pension Homeland

O **D** Buitenzwembad Marineterrein

KATTENBURGERSTRAAT

OOSTELIJKE EILANDEN

CEZAR PETERSTRAAT

D Hiding in Plain Sight

CENTRUM

D Café de Druif

Bakers & Roasters **E** **E**

A Het Rembrandthuis

A

S

JODENBUURT

Episode   **S** Kilo Store

Café Kadijk

OOSTENBURGERGRACHT

Nieuwevaart

HOOGTE KADIJK

Entrepotdok

A

S Waterloopleinmarkt

A Verzetsmuseum

A Muziektheater Amsterdam Museum

A Jewish Historical Museum

PLANTAGE-BUURT

A Artis Micropia

D Brouwerij 't IJ

N Mooie Boules

ZEEBURGERDIJK

A **E** Dignita Hoftuin

SARPHATISTRAAT

Singelgracht

A Museum van de Geest

PLANTAGE MIDDENLAAN

WEESPERSTRAAT

WEESPER-BUURT

N EasyLaughs

COMMELINSTRAAT

Amstel

A Royal Theatre Carré

A Filmtheater Kriterion

Tropenmuseum **A**

EERSTE VAN SWINDENSTRAAT

SARPHATISTRAAT

MAURITSKADE

S Dappermarkt

WIBAUTSTRAAT

BOERHAAVE-PLEIN

'S-GRAVESANDE-PLEIN

O Oosterpark

OOSTERPARK

OOST

LINNAEUSSTRAAT

POLDERWEG

WEESPERZIJDE

D 4850

E Hartog's Volkoren

2e OOSTER PARK STR.

D Coffee Bru

OUD-OOST

POPULIERENWEG

S. BIKO-PLEIN

AMSTELDIJK

VAN WOUSTRAAT

Amstel

N Canvas

KRUGER-PLEIN

Ringvaart

N Le Perr

MIDDENWEG

E De Ka

KAMERLINGH ONNESLAAN

Park Frankendael

D Dakterras GAPP

0 metres 500
0 yards 500

MAP 4

0 metres 500
0 yards 500

BUIKSLOOT

Buiksloterbreek

NDSM

NDSM-PLEIN

Ⓢ IJ-Hallen

METAALBEWERKERWEG

KLAPROZENWEG

BUIKSLOTERDIJK

FLORADORP

BUIKSLOTERHAM

RIDDERSPOORWEG

KLAPROZENWEG

KAMPERFOELIEWEG

SNEEUWBALSTR.

NOORD

Noorderpark
Ⓞ

WINGERDWEG

DISTELWEG

RIBESSTR.

Noordhollandskanaal

Café de Ceuvel Ⓓ

GRASWEG

ASTERWEG

Ⓐ Nxt Museum

MOS-
PLEIN

J. VAN HASSELTWEG

Het IJ

LUPINE-
PLEIN

Buiksloterkanaal

VAN DER PEKSTRAAT

HAGEDOORNWEG

LEEUWARDERWEG

ADELAARSWEG

Fromagerie Abraham Ⓢ

OVERHOEKS

NIEUWE

MEEUWENLAAN

BUIKSLOTERWEG

Comedy Café Ⓝ

EYE Ⓐ
Filmmuseum

Ⓓ The Coffee Virus
Ⓝ Shelter
Ⓝ The Butcher Social Club

Oedipus Ⓓ
Brewing

DE RUIJTERKADE

Tolhuistuin Ⓝ

IJPLEIN

NOORDWAL

Het IJ

Amsterdam Centraal to
Haarlem Bike Ride Ⓞ Ⓞ Amsterdam Centraal to
Durgerdam Bike Ride

Ⓢ I Amsterdam
Store

CENTRUM

STATIONS-
PLEIN

PIET HEINKADE

MAP 5

5

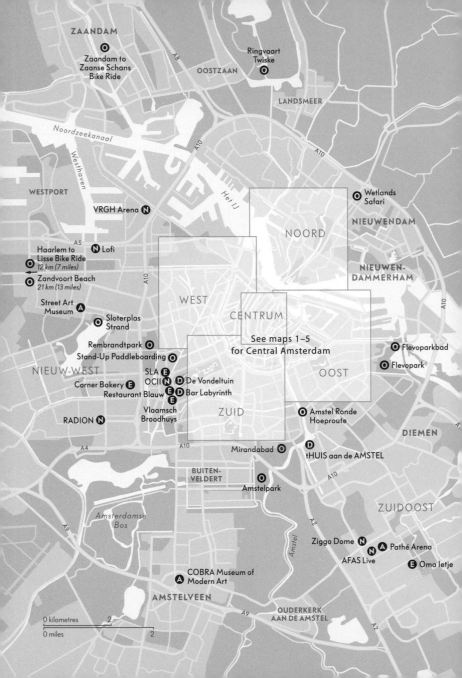

ZAANDAM

Zaandam to
Zaanse Schans
Bike Ride

A8

OOSTZAAN

Ringvaart
Twiske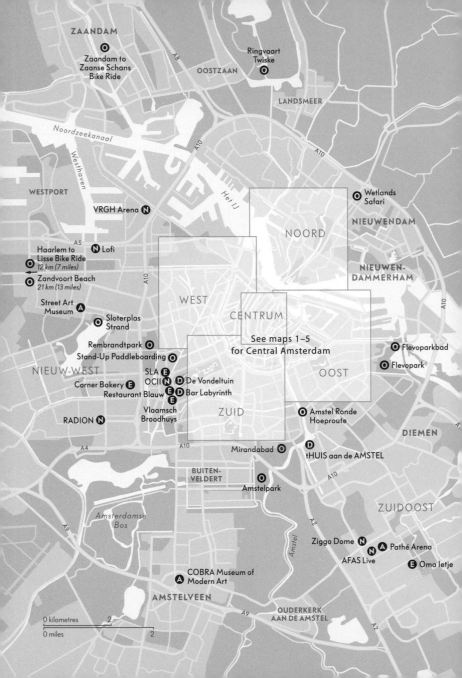

LANDSMEER

A10

Noordzeekanaal

Westhaven

A10

Het IJ

Wetlands
Safari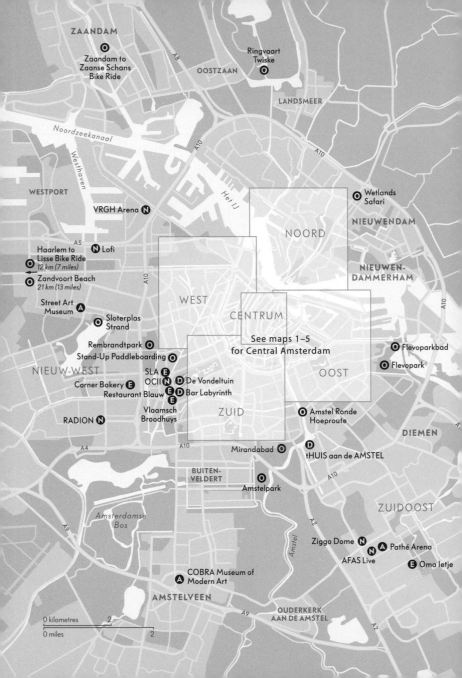

NOORD

NIEUWENDAM

WESTPORT

VRGH Arena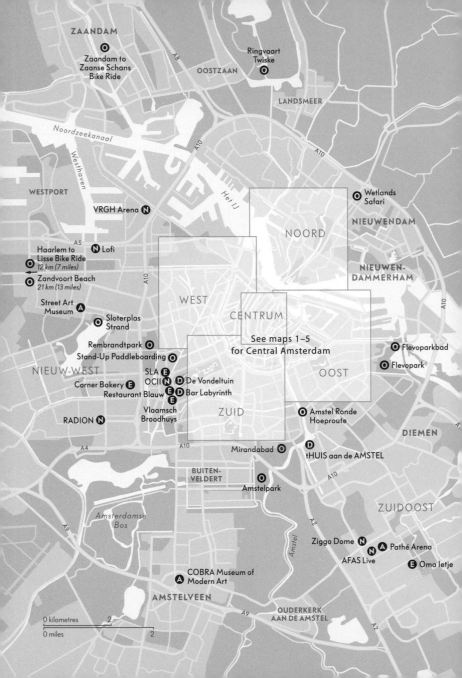

NIEUWEN-
DAMMERHAM

A5

Lofi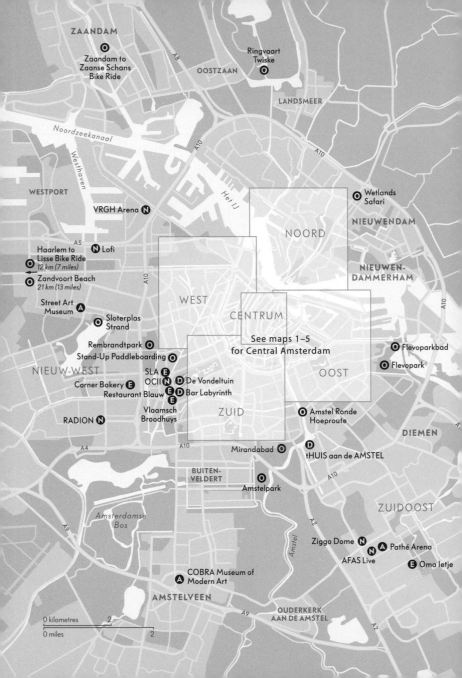

Haarlem to
Lisse Bike Ride
12 km (7 miles)

Zandvoort Beach
21 km (13 miles)

A10

WEST

CENTRUM

See maps 1–5
for Central Amsterdam

Flevoparkbad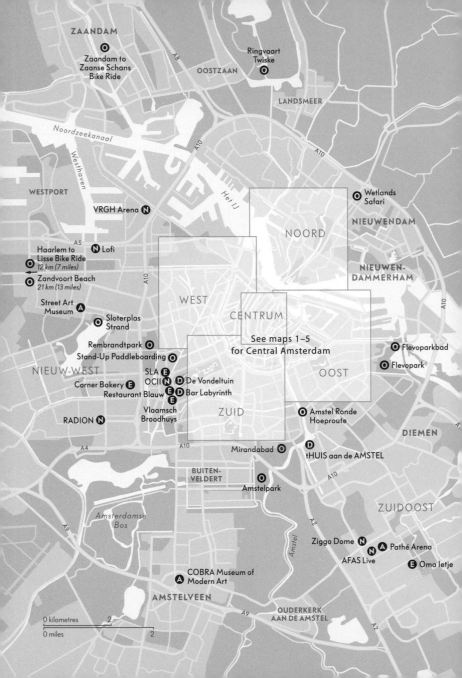

Flevopark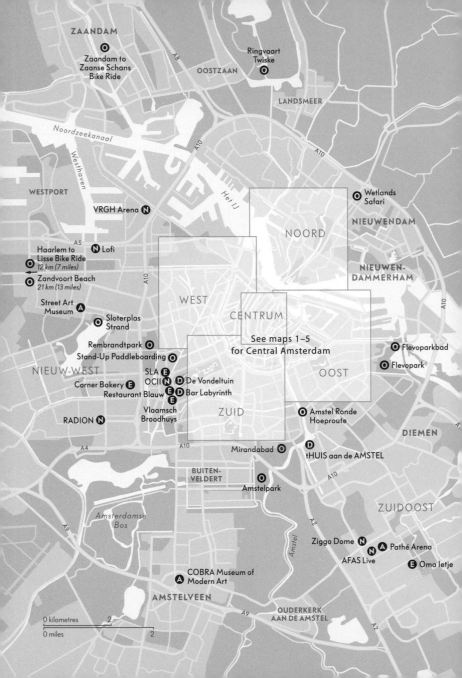

Street Art
Museum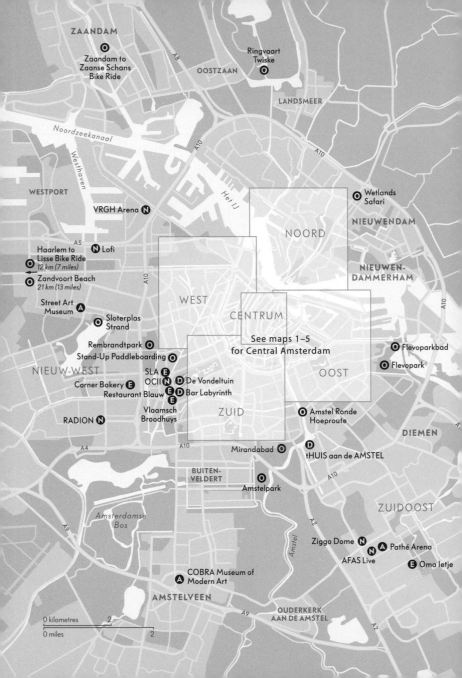

Sloterplas
Strand

Rembrandtpark

Stand-Up Paddleboarding

SLA
OCII

De Vondeltuin

OOST

NIEUW-WEST

Corner Bakery

Restaurant Blauw

Bar Labyrinth

Vlaamsch
Broodhuys

RADION

ZUID

Amstel Ronde
Hoeproute

DIEMEN

A4

A10

Mirandabad

tHUIS aan de AMSTEL

BUITEN-
VELDERT

Amstelpark

A10

ZUIDOOST

Amsterdamse
Bos

A9

Amstel

A2

Ziggo Dome

AFAS Live

Pathé Arena

Oma Ietje

COBRA Museum of
Modern Art

AMSTELVEEN

A9

OUDERKERK
AAN DE AMSTEL

A2

0 kilometres   2

0 miles   2

MAP 6

EAT

Munch on a stroopwafel at a street market, devour a spicy roti on the go or feast on Dutch pancakes – Amsterdam offers many culinary delights, no matter your mood.

Brunch Spots

This isn't just a meal. Brunch in Amsterdam is the social highlight of any weekend, where friends gather over stacks of pancakes and plates of avocado on toast to catch up on all the week's news.

TEDS

Map 3; Bosboom Tuissantstraat 60, Oud-West;
///scars.lump.quicker; www.teds-place.nl

All hail TEDS, one of the first places in Amsterdam to do brunch all day, all week. The locals still can't get enough of this place, with its airy, modern interior and truly decadent menu. And you'll likely worship it, too; if you love butter and bacon, and like the sound of pancakes topped with Nutella and Oreos, you've found your new spiritual home.

DE BAKKERSWINKEL

Map 2; Polonceaukade 1&2, Westerpark;
///dragons.ports.sigh; www.debakkerswinkelwestergas.nl

Just try to get through a meal here without gasping "yum" every 30 seconds. This local-turned-national treasure tips its hat to Britain with its sweet scones – bested only by the savoury versions. There are three locations in Amsterdam but nothing beats tucking into a hearty

If you don't mind sharing your eggs, cheese and bacon, order a great-value breakfast for two.

breakfast (think fried eggs and crispy bacon with an obligatory side of scones) at this lofty outpost, which is backed by the families who call Westerpark home.

DIGNITA HOFTUIN

Map 4; Nieuwe Herengracht 8a, Plantagebuurt;
///grain.computer.dreams; www.eatwelldogood.nl/dignita-hoftuin

This secret spot is one that Amsterdammers like to save for themselves – so don't tell them we sent you. Tucked away off traffic-clogged Weesperstraat you'll find this all-day brunch café plopped in the heart of a pretty little garden. On sunny days, pals sit out on the patio, soaking up the scenery and chatting over their virtuous avocado salads and root veggie fritters. When the weather is iffy, they retreat inside to watch the rain over a comforting plate of apple pie. Delightful.

BAKERS & ROASTERS

Map 4; Kadijksplein 16, Plantagebuurt;
///spring.arrive.clauses; www.bakersandroasters.com

Bakers & Roasters may have some of the best poached eggs in the city, but one look at the other plates on the tables around you and you'd be forgiven for jumping ship. The French toast made from syrupy slabs of banana nut bread, stacks of blueberry pancakes and nutty homemade granola turn everybody's eyes.

» **Don't leave without** trying the spicy huevos rancheros, best paired with an ice-cold glass of mango juice.

OMELEGG

Map 3; Ferdinand Bolstraat 143, De Pijp;
///swim.nimbly.drove; www.omelegg.com

Big night out? Feeling a tad worse for wear? Consider Omelegg your new secret weapon, thanks to its vast and restorative egg-themed menu. We're talking omelettes made with every added ingredient you can think of (no, seriously) plus a smattering of brunch favourites, like shakshuka. On the rare occasion you don't find what you're looking for, ask the waiter to whip you up your eggs whichever way you like.

LITTLE COLLINS

Map 3; Eerste Sweelinckstraat 19F, De Pijp;
///repeated.bugs.decreased; www.littlecollins.nl

The best things come in small packages. Take Little Collins, seemingly plucked from the streets of Melbourne with its wooden tables, jugs of freshly picked flowers and battalions of wine bottles lining the

Shh!

For Oost neighbourhood locals in the know The Cottage (*www.thecottage.amsterdam*) is the only place worth stopping in for a homely omelette or scrambled eggs brunch. Sit on the cosy cushions in one of the huge windows and see what all the fuss is about, then take a post-brunch break in the equally unknown Oostpoort shopping centre across the street. It's prime window-gazing territory.

walls (all of which isn't surprising given the owner's Aussie roots). This nook of a restaurant is always abuzz on weekend mornings, when trendy young locals catch up over Bloody Marys and dishes like buckwheat galettes or burrata and figs on sourdough.

MOAK PANCAKES

Map 2; De Clercqstraat 34, Oud-West;
///other.pumpkin.impact; www.moakpancakes.nl

Some say it's sacrilege, but there's no denying that Moak's thick American-style pancakes have found their footing alongside their typically thinner Dutch cousins. This is all thanks to founders Sten and Sammy. Whipping up these fluffy delicacies with a flurry of healthy ingredients — each stack uses wholegrain flour, zero added sugar and organic buttermilk — the pair have made it far too easy for Amsterdammers to brush off traditions. Whichever topping you pick, expect them in epic proportions.

» Don't leave without ordering The Ice Cube, a vegan pancake topped with a scoop of saffron pistachio ice cream and Canadian maple syrup.

CUT THROAT BARBER & COFFEE

Map 1; Beursplein 5, Dam; ///patrol.saloons.settle; www.cutthroatbarber.nl

Okay, it's not an eggs-and-avo kind of a brunch place, but Cut Throat is no ordinary spot. Caribbean street food is served until 9pm (find us another brunch menu that lasts that long), the bar pours tipples to its cool, tattooed patrons until 2am at weekends and a barbershop keeps Amsterdammers looking fresh. What more could you ask for?

Fresh Bakeries

Amsterdammers buy fresh bread daily, so it comes as no surprise that the bakery plays a vital role in local life. Here, you'll find all manner of baked goods that run the gamut from stroopwafels *to macaroons.*

GEBROEDERS NIEMEIJER

Map 1; Nieuwendijk 35, Grachtengordel;
///monitors.resist.incomes; www.gebroedersniemeijer.nl

When brothers Marco and Issa struggled to find a good artisanal French bakery in Amsterdam, they started up this fine place – and now they're considered among the best bread makers in the city. The simple tearoom is the go-to for a classic *petit déjeuner*, complete with buttery croissants, fresh *tartelettes* and homemade jams that you'll want to stock up on.

HARTOG'S VOLKOREN

Map 4; Wibautstraat 77, Oud-Oost;
///request.exams.gangway; www.volkorenbrood.nl

Run by the Hartog family since 1896, this bakery has long held a place in local hearts for its wholewheat specialist breads. And the recipes and philosophy of founder Aagje Hartog are alive and well:

During the winter *oliebollen* (similar to doughnuts) are freshly baked by the Hartogs in front of their store.

this remains the only bakery in the city that mills its own flour. Join the queue to pick up a delicious sandwich or cake — it's worth the wait.

LE FOURNIL DE SÉBASTIEN

Map 3; Olympiaplein 119, Oud-Zuid;
///putter.cakes.explains; www.lefournil.nl

The aromas of piping hot *chaussons aux pommes* and *pains au chocolat* welcome you as soon as you step inside this classic bakery. You can be sure of a great baguette too, but it's the patisserie offerings made by French baker extraordinaire Sébastien Roturier and his Dutch wife Susan that make this place shine.

CORNER BAKERY

Map 6; Koningin Wilhelminaplein 60–62, Nieuw-West;
///noodle.supporter.spit; www.cornerbakeryamsterdam.com

Sure, traditional bakeries have their place, but Corner Bakery is all about being over-the-top. Brioche French toast bursts with fresh fruit and maple syrup, the homemade vegan pie is a cheesecake, carrot cake, apple pie and red velvet cake in one, and the sandwich rolls are overflowing with fillings. After all, the bakery's walls are emblazoned with the slogan "We live by one rule... calories don't count when you are at Corner Bakery." Is that so? Sign us up.

» **Don't leave without** trying a hot freakshake: a rainbow shake topped with marshmallow fluff.

LANSKROON BAKERY

Map 1; Singel 385, Grachtengordel;
///alleges.gain.adopting; www.lanskroon.nl

If Amsterdammers had their own national dish, it would be the
stroopwafel, a chewy waffle filled with gooey caramel. One of the
few places still handbaking this much-loved sweet is Lanskroon, run
by the same family for over 100 years. Treat yourself in its teeny-tiny
tearoom: one bite into a king-sized *stroopwafel* (it barely fits into
one hand), and you'll never buy a pre-packaged one again.

LE PERRON

Map 4; Middenweg 59, Watergraafsmeer;
///hammer.improve.proposes; www.leperron.nl

Descended from a family of bakers, siblings Robin and Sanne
have reinvented the traditional bakery with a focus on organic,
pure ingredients. Wooden barrels overflow with multigrain
sourdough and rye loaves, nutritious spelt and kamut breads
packed with seeds, and nut and cinnamon buns. There's also
gluten-free muffins for those who steer clear of wheat.

VLAAMSCH BROODHUYS

Map 6; Amstelveenseweg 176–178, Oud-Zuid;
///connects.informal.gliders; www.vlaamschbroodhuys.nl

The words "chain bakery" may give Amsterdammers the shudders,
but the homely feel of this branch will fool you into thinking it's a
unique neighbourhood bakery. Buzzing with families every morning,

it draws crowds for its fresh-from-the-oven sourdough bread – a speciality of Dutch owners Dimitri and Diante Roels. The menu brims with gourmet sandwiches, delicious cheese melts and healthy salads, too.

» **Don't leave without** ordering the *kaasragoutbroodje* (cheese ragout pastry), flaky on the outside and creamy on the inside.

IAMBE
Map 3; Van der Helstplein 6, De Pijp; ///fluid.grit.cheeses; www.raphaelstichting.org/iambe

Run by the Raphaël Foundation healthcare provider, iambe is both a bakery and a social workplace for young people with intellectual disabilities. It has a laudable aim and super-friendly vibes – staff always remember your name – but these aren't the only reasons that locals rave about it. Regulars claim this spot has the best *saucijzenbroodje* (pigs in a blanket) in Amsterdam.

STACH
Map 3; Van Woustraat 154, De Pijp; ///divisions.installed.impulses; www.stach-food.nl

The De Pijp branch of this small deli is a neighbourhood favourite. Office workers stop by en route to work, picking up a fruit juice and freshly baked banana bread or, if it's looking like a tough day, a few tasty pastries. Later on, students (drawn by the Stach's cheap prices) pop in between study sessions for psychedelic meringues and comforting wood-oven pizzas.

Cheap Eats

Despite the city's rising prices, restaurants serving good food for good value aren't too hard to come by. Follow the locals to their favourite bargain bites and your money will go a lot further.

CAFÉ KADIJK

Map 4; Kadijksplein 5, Plantagebuurt;
///speeches.tasters.relating; www.cafekadijk.nl

While students are taken to traditional Indonesian restaurants by their families to celebrate their graduation with elaborate "rice tables", they take themselves to Café Kadijk for the pared-down version (in size and price, not flavour) simply to celebrate dinnertime. The small plates of hot spicy dishes (a Dutch take on Indonesian cooking) include such favourites as lamb satay and spicy mackerel.

FRENS HARINGHANDEL

Map 1; Koningsplein, Grachtengordel;
///concerts.open.beaker; www.frens-haring.nl.en

It's hard to miss Frens Haringhandel: every day sees long lines of regulars queuing for the fresh-from-the-sea herring, served raw with a generous sprinkling of onions. Just as popular is the

The best time to try the herring is just after the new herring release in June and July.

kibbeling — deep-fried battered chunks of cod that taste oh-so-good. A household name in the city since 1972, this family-run fish stand has stood the test of time.

SEOUL FOOD

Map 2; Kinkerstraat 73A, Oud-West;
///suppose.lungs.seat; www.seoulfoodamsterdam.nl

Lose yourself in K-pop tunes as you walk through the door of this Korean café and takeaway. After deciding what to order from the huge choice of unbelievably cheap bibimbap, rice rolls and kimchi offerings, join the hipster lunch crowd at the communal table (if you can find a space) or grab your takeaway box to go. Everything's super fresh and once it's gone it's gone, so get here early.

» Don't leave without browsing the shop at the back, with its eclectic collection of Korean snacks and knick-knacks.

CAFÉ DE TUIN

Map 2; Tweede Tuindwarsstraat 13, Jordaan;
///glitz.weaned.abruptly; www.cafedetuin.nl

There are few better places for a cosy *borrel* (the supremely Dutch art of having an evening drink and nibbles over a catch-up with mates) than this brown pub. But it's the legendary *bitterballen* that we're here for. These classic, crunchy, roasting-hot golden-brown meat balls, made with a traditional beef ragu recipe, are a favourite snack to soak up those beers.

RAM'S ROTI

Map 2; Jan van Galenstraat 107, F, De Baarsjes;
///intervals.flies.officers; www.ramstroti.nl

Hungry office workers have one thing in mind when it's time for
lunch: tasty, no-fuss rotis from this Surinamese takeaway. Join
them in the queue and choose from the huge variety of succulent,
curry-flavoured meat or vegan fillings. Then, grab your flatbread to
go and head opposite to Erasmus Park for a picnic.

HAP-HMM

Map 3; Eerste Helmersstraat 33, Oud-West;
///panther.runways.took; www.hap-hmm.nl

Want a taste of Dutch cuisine without spending a pretty penny?
Seek out Hap-Hmm. This intimate Dutch diner feels more like a
family living room than a renowned restaurant: home-cooked meals
like "grandma's meatballs" line the menu and staff welcome you
like you're part of the family. Be sure to book ahead – this place
is too good to miss.

OMA IETJE

Map 6; Heesterveld 3, Zuidoost;
///competent.gliders.most; www.omaietje.nl

Not many tourists make their way this far west, but those who do
are well rewarded. This lovely laidback café promises some of the
city's best grilled cheese sandwiches, not to mention delicious
vegan dishes. Sit outside in the sun with a plant-based cappuccino

and some honest lunch grub and you'll wonder why you didn't venture this way sooner.

>> **Don't leave without** exploring the surrounding area — within the colourfully painted buildings lie numerous artist studios and co-working spaces for the city's creatives.

WARUNG SPANG MAKANDRA

Map 3; Gerard Doustraat 39, De Pijp;
///nozzles.flown.powerful; www.spangmakandra.nl

This Amsterdam institution, one of the oldest Surinamese joints in the city, champions three things: good food, good value and good company. And with delicious fusion dishes, budget prices and friendly staff, it never fails to hit the mark. Arrive early to beat the crowds and don't be tempted to over-order (serving sizes here are *really* good value for money).

Shh!

Hidden away in the African-Caribbean Zuidoost borough is the cavernous World of Food (www.worldoffoodamsterdam. nl). This food hall brings together cooks from all over the world, serving unpretentious dishes from home. The minute you walk through the doors, Surinamese barbecued meat fills the air, wafting with the scent of Pakistani karahi and unmistakable Thai tom yum kung. It's the best way to go on an inexpensive culinary journey to far-flung parts of the world.

Comfort Food

*When the weather doesn't play nice, family and friends
seek out the perfect remedy to the rain: cosying up in
beloved restaurants to feast on warming stews,
indulgent pancakes and perfect pizzas.*

UMAIMON

Map 3; Korte Leidsedwarsstraat 51, Leidseplein;
///cute.staging.dangerously; www.umaimonramennoodle.nl

Bamboo lanterns, manga posters and a lively *izakaya* vibe set
the scene for the only restaurant worth visiting in touristy
Leidseplein. Owned by chef Haruhiko Saeki, Umaimon is the
home of Sapporo-style chicken ramen; go for the signature
special – the thick, flavourful soup will transport you straight to
the back alleys of Saeki's home city.

LALIBELA

Map 3; Eerste Helmersstraat 249, Overtoombuurt, Oud-West;
///winner.live.dodges; www.lalibela.nl

Ethiopian food has made great waves in Amsterdam, and in a sea
of Ethiopian restaurants this is arguably the best. The music and
decor are a backdrop to friends piling in for the *injera* topped with

rich, fragrant stews. Bring clean hands (your utensils) and empty bellies, and opt for one of the combi-menus of small sharing plates, washed down with fruity beers served in gourds.

» **Don't leave without** a tasty traditional Ethiopian coffee after your meal. From flavour to texture, it's really something else.

SHAM OOST
Map 4; Borneo Steiger 1, Oostelijk Havengebied;
///skis.wheels.talking; www.restaurantsham.nl

When Syrian refugees arrived in Amsterdam in 2017, Mumen al-Azhar helped some of his fellow countrymen and women adjust to their new home by employing them in his restaurant. Here they cook up falafel, *fattoush*, grilled aubergines and skewered meats, drawing crowds craving the taste of home. (The 360-degree water views from the mini-lake location are a bonus.)

HEMELSE MODDER
Map 1; Oude Waal 11, De Wallen;
///kings.soldiers.shrimp; www.hemelsemodder.nl

When long work days are nearing the end, young professionals have one place in mind: this smart dining room, where modern Dutch dishes (think crispy potato biscuit with kohlrabi cream) make perfect comfort food. Some of the ingredients may be tough to translate, but you'll walk away with a new understanding of the word *lekker* (scrumptious) – especially if you try the restaurant's namesake dish: a "heavenly mud" chocolate mousse.

Solo, Pair, Crowd

Sometimes all you want is a steak dinner. Whether it's you, two or the whole crew, Amsterdam has you covered.

FLYING SOLO
Befriend the bar staff

The staff at Leidseplein ribs restaurant Café de Klos have enough banter to keep your ears as entertained as your taste buds. And arriving alone means you won't have to wait long for a bar-side seat.

IN A PAIR
Oysters for two

Want to impress a date? Take them to Panache in Oud-West. The drool-worthy surf-and-turf menu pairs perfectly with a dark jungle interior, and the cocktails will make you want to linger.

FOR A CROWD
Fondue fun

Join other groups of friends at Het Karbeel in De Wallen for two things: fabulous steak in pepper sauce and cheese fondue, usually together. The 16th-century building is a cosy, warm spot for a get-together.

FULU MANDARIJN

Map 1; Rokin 26, De Wallen; ///trendy.beaters.drag; www.fulumandarijn.com

Ask any Chinese Amsterdammer where to find the best Sichuan food and they'll direct you to this gem. Inside, hot plates sizzle with red peppercorn steak, clay teapots spin on turntables and a loyal clientele tuck into dishes like spicy *Chongqing* chicken. This is the real deal.

EATMOSFERA

Map 3; Korte Reguliersdwarsstraat 8, Grachtengordel;
///lanes.delved.rinses; www.eatmosfera.nl

Are these the best Italian pizzas in the city? Let the debate begin. Many say that the pizzas could be straight out of a Roman pizzeria so it's no surprise that Eatmosfera is such a big hit with the Italian community. There are tasty pastas too, but if your dinner isn't baked in a wood oven, you're going to find yourself with serious sourdough envy.

» Don't leave without heading around the corner to Pathé Tuschinski *(p127)*; Eatmosfera is the perfect place for a pre-cinema dinner.

PANNENKOEKENHUIS UPSTAIRS

Map 1; Grimburgwal 2, De Wallen;
///coupler.danger.slower; www.upstairspannenkoeken.nl

This tiny hidey hole of a pancake house is known colloquially as "Upstairs Pancakes" because, well, it's upstairs. And not just any stairs – creaky, near vertical stairs. But it's worth crawling up to the second floor for plate-sized Dutch pancakes (sweet or savoury). Be sure to get here before lunchtime – when the batter runs out, the kitchen closes.

Veggie & Vegan

With every local who goes meat-free, it seems like a great new veggie or vegan restaurant pops up to satiate them. No wonder, then, Amsterdammers call their city a veggie Valhalla.

VEGAN JUNK FOOD BAR

Map 3; Reguliersdwarsstraat 57, Grachtengordel; ///maker.hacking.areas; www.veganjunkfoodbar.com

Rainbow loaded fries and burgers with pink buns: this isn't junk food like you know it. VJFB serves up some of the tastiest (and most colourful) vegan cuisine in the town, and locals can't get enough. You'll find four branches in Amsterdam alone, with more set to open across Europe. To put it simply, these folks are fuelling the vegan revolution, and it's time for you to join the cause.

MEATLESS DISTRICT

Map 2; Bilderdijkstraat 65–67, Oud-West; ///audio.arts.liners; www.meatlessdistrict.com

It says a lot about this place that most of the well-heeled diners aren't full-time vegans. That's down to the allure of the Meatless District's ever-changing, 100 per cent vegan menu. Eager young

 Looking to buy vegan ingredients? The Vegan Fresco De Baarsjes supermarket is around the corner.

waitstaff dish out the stuff of comfort cravings, all made from local produce and dressed up bistro style, ideally paired with a cocktail or vegan wine.

MEDIAMATIC
Map 4; Dijksgracht 6, Oostelijke Eilanden;
///similar.silly.mostly; www.mediamatic.net

Part of the Mediamatic art and science centre, this glasshouse restaurant serves up a five-course menu that makes liberal use of the vegetables and herbs sustainably grown in the on-site garden and greenhouse. Every night the chefs prepare something different, blending flavours to create delicious concoctions, which guests tuck into with their hands. Food doesn't get fresher than this.

>> Don't leave without asking about the regular workshops on everything from making kimchi to creating perfume.

BONBOON
Map 2; Rozenstraat 12, Jordaan;
///furnish.genetics.output; www.bonboon.nl

A charming location in Jordaan; cosy tables in a small dining room that oozes charm; fragrant, inventive combinations of vegetables and grains on an ever-changing menu. It's no wonder that this café, born out of owner Daphne Althoff's dream to bring delicious non-animal food to Amsterdam's citizens, is always full of foodies – vegan or otherwise (so try to plan your visit a week ahead).

DE WAAGHALS

Map 3; Frans Halstraat 29, De Pijp;
///compound.deed.opinion; www.waaghals.nl

You know those people who say they could never be veggie because they don't like fake meat? Bring them here. Not an ounce of fake meat in sight, and the place is packed with carnivores taking a day off. De Waaghals prefers to let the local crops and cheeses shine: super-tasty ingredients that don't pretend to be anything other than what they are.

GOLDEN TEMPLE

Map 3; Utrechtsestraat 126, Grachtengordel; ///evaded.double.range;
www.restaurantgoldentemple.com

Had a busy day exploring? Wander into this welcoming Indian rest-aurant and you'll feel a weight off your shoulders. Inside, friends feast on filling curries in cushion-packed nooks, while couples share tasty garlic naans on the sofas. It's the perfect place for a veggie recharge.

SLA

Map 6; Amstelveenseweg 124, Oud-Zuid;
///fixtures.unwind.truck; www.ilovesla.com

Don't be put off by the queue of office workers at this salad bar chain, there's a good reason they've all come here for lunch. Quick, healthy and packed with flavour, SLA's sustainably sourced salad bowls are the stuff of veggie dreams.

» Don't leave without asking about SLA's salad-focused cookbook; the recipes inside will have you whipping up the good stuff in no time.

Liked by the locals

"We want to let people experience
how tasty plant-based meals are.
With healthy food that's not
too complicated, SLA
highlights the origin of
the ingredients."

NINA AND JOP, OWNERS OF SLA

Special Occasion

Celebrating your graduation? A big birthday? Or just fancy a Friday night treat? Amsterdam's got every celebration covered, with inventive spots that embody the city's creative and multicultural spirit.

RESTAURANT BLAUW

Map 6; Amstelveenseweg 158–160, Oud-Zuid;
///curry.burn.building; www.restaurantblauw.nl

Chattering families and friends gather to celebrate over Blauw's *rijsttafel* (rice table). This huge spread of Indonesian small side dishes like spicy braised beef, shrimp satay and grilled aubergine and beans, all served with heaps of rice, is perfect for sharing. New to Indonesian street food? You can count on the speedy, friendly waiters to help you assemble the perfect festive meal.

YAMAZATO

Map 3; Ferdinand Bolstraat 333, De Pijp;
///koala.gulped.nothing; www.yamazato.nl

Celebrating a splurge-worthy work promotion? Dine like a Japanese emperor at Yamazato. Donning their finest, diners come here for exquisite, delicate *kaiseki* (haute Japanese) feasts, all cooked up by chefs who have undergone years of traditional training in Japan. For a price, of course: nearly €300 for a full dinner with wine and sake pairings, with simpler lunch options starting at €60. If your wallet can take it, it's an experience you'll be talking about years later.

» Don't leave without heading to the bar on the 23rd floor of the hotel for some cocktail action with a view.

BREDA

Map 1; Singel 210, Grachtengordel; ///emblem.rank.pads; www.bredagroup-amsterdam.com

Rich, satisfying meals enjoyed at leisure in rustic surroundings. That's just what restaurant Breda's team grew up enjoying in North Brabant (Breda is a city in this southern Dutch province), and they've imported these same principles to their restaurant in the national capital. Celebrate that big anniversary over a plate of pork belly, rib-eye steak or mussels. No one ever eats here just once.

SALMUERA

Map 2; Rozengracht 106, Jordaan; ///began.activity.manual; www.sal-amsterdam.nl

Locals don't go to the rash of touristy Argentinian steakhouses taking up prime real estate in the party districts. Instead, when a craving for *chimichurri* strikes, they make for Salmuera. Here two Argentinian-Dutch brothers dish out pan-Latin American fusion favourites in a swanky, moody dining room. Tequila fans, take note: the bar is ready to provide a full mezcal re-education.

LOS PILONES

Map 1; Geldersekade 111, Nieuwmarkt;
///instant.bunkers.dads; www.lospilones.com

The staff at this festive favourite know how to keep their customers jolly: goblets of flavoured margaritas will land on your table just about as quickly as you can order them. But the food is the real star of the show, a selection of more Mex-Mex than Tex-Mex headliners. Celebrate with your friends inside or out on the terrace.

DE KAS

Map 4; Kamerlingh Onneslaan 3, Watergraafsmeer;
///moats.mining.castle; www.restaurantdekas.com

This chic restaurant is *the* place for an intimate, laid-back date. Guests are greeted by floor-to-ceiling glass panels that open up to vistas of landscaped gardens, a water fountain and the lush greenery of Frankendael Park. The farm-to-table menu is all about fresh produce grown in the restaurant's very own nursery, a perfect pairing with those leafy nature views.

Try it!
LEARN TO FORAGE

Fancy a stroll with your date before eating at De Kas? Forage for local seasonal herbs together on an Urban Herbology guided walk *(www.urbanherbology.org)* in the adjoining Frankendael Park.

LASTAGE

Map 1; Geldersekade 29, Nieuwmarkt;
///fuss.cones.leader; www.restaurantlastage.nl

No disrespect, but chef Rogier van Dam doesn't want visitors to his Dutch-French restaurant to stiffen up when they see it's got a Michelin star (so he's hung it in the basement), or expect to be slammed by the bill (prices really are very reasonable). Still, Michelin rules year after year that the quality is undeniable. Bring your in-laws or a foodie you want to impress, choose from a menu of twelve dishes (which might include terrine of red mullet, cod with bacon and oyster sauce or pork tenderloin) and let the staff do the rest.

» Don't leave without opting in on the wine pairings – they're central to the dining concept, and full of delightful surprises whether you're a wine newbie or certified expert.

HOOGTIJ

Map 5; Johan van Hasseltweg 39, Nieuwendammerham;
///copy.remember.doctors; www.hoogtij.amsterdam

Gob-smacking city and river views, original food, live jazz – all in a rooftop garden. If that sounds like your ideal setting for a party, you need to bring the gang here. And, oh, what a night you'll all have. A changing line-up of local chefs prep street-food inspired dishes, live performers provide a peppy soundtrack and the city itself supplies the scenery. If the weather doesn't hold up (this is Amsterdam, after all), everyone decamps to the glasshouse – no spirits dampened here. HoogtIJ's events are irregular, so for details of what's afoot, always check Facebook.

A foodie morning in
Oud-West

In a city churning out delicious plate of food after delicious plate of food, Oud-West is the place to go for some of the best. Spurred on by the neighbourhood's multicultural inhabitants, this former industrial area has foodie hotspots galore, including the seriously swish tram depot-turned food court De Foodhallen and the long-running favourite Ten Katemarkt. There's no better way to spend a morning than filling up on flavour-packed treats as you wander the area.

1. Waldo Chocolade & Patisserie
Elandsgracht 91, Jordaan;
www.waldopatisserie.nl
///shipped.create.detect

2. Kookstudio Keizer Culinair
Elandsstraat 169–173,
Jordaan; www.keizer
culinair.nl
///jeering.smashes.dream

3. Toko Bersama
Bilderdijkstraat 116,
Oud-West;
www.tokobersama.nl
///discrepancy.journey.boring

4. De Foodhallen
Bellamyplein 51,
Oud-West;
www.foodhallen.nl
///private.snaps.fountain

Ten Katemarkt
///vampire.milder.bronzed

WES

Kostverlorenvaart

OUD-WEST

End with lunch at DE FOODHALLEN
Follow your nose as you walk through this large food hall. Try Vietnamese bowls at Viet View or Dutch *bitterballen* at De Ballenbar. Finish with a local beer at Beer Bar.

Running since 1912, **Ten Katemarkt** *is a local gem, offering everything from fresh produce to Nepali street food.*

Get cooking at
KOOKSTUDIO
KEIZER CULINAIR

Join a cookery class or workshop at this famous Dutch culinary school, where you can tune up your cooking skills and dabble in all sorts of cuisines.

Snack at
TOKO BERSAMA

A local favourite for takeaway Indonesian food, Toko Bersama is the best spot in Oud-West to try a *loempia* (spring roll) or *pisang goreng* (fried plantain). Grab your snack and enjoy it by the Bilderdijkgracht canal.

Have breakfast at
WALDO CHOCOLADE
& PATISSERIE

Start the day by filling up on tantalizing homemade pastries and aromatic artisan coffee at this French-inspired patisserie.

JORDAAN

CENTRUM

ROZENGRACHT

Kattensloot

NASSAUKADE

PRINSENGRACHT

ELANDSSTR.

HAZENSTR.

ELANDSGR.

Singelgracht

LIJNBAANSGRACHT

Lijnbaansgracht

Prinsengracht

RAAM-
PLEIN

BILDERDIJKSTR.

KINKERSTRAAT

Bilderdijkgracht

Jacob

van

Lennepkanaal

NASSAUKADE

LEIDSE-
PLEIN

1E CONSTANTIJN HUYGENSSTRAAT

OVERTOOM

1

2

3

0 metres   200
0 yards   200

DRINK

*Meeting for **borreltijd** (drinks and snacks) with friends is a ritual. Beers are clinked after work, wine is sipped on date night and coffee is drunk at all hours.*

Breweries

With a brewing history going back centuries,
Amsterdam offers many a finely crafted local beer.
The heavenly homegrown hops come in every flavour
and colour to satisfy this city of beer drinkers.

BIERFABRIEK

Map 1; Nes 67, De Wallen;
///shadows.rental.sheep; www.bierfabriek.com

The Beer Factory may brew only three beers (Rosso, Nero and Puur
Pilsner) on site, but it does them to perfection. Round up your mates
and gather around the tables, which handily have built-in taps to
pour your own pints against a backdrop of chrome-and-copper casks.

BROUWERIJ 'T IJ

Map 4; Funenkade 7, Plantagebuurt;
///press.unto.prom; www.brouwerijhetij.nl

Don't worry about pronouncing the name, everyone just calls
this place "the windmill brewery" – spot the city's last wooden
windmill towering above it. Lines of Amsterdammers form inside the
small bar, collecting the city's OG craft beers by the stein. Out on
the terrace, rows of picnic tables and any spare patch of pavement

are mobbed by a hodgepodge of young locals – anyone who can sneak out of work early (last orders is at 8pm). Which beer to start with? The well-hopped, strong Columbus amber ale is a popular choice with local beer aficionados.

»» Don't leave without booking a tour to learn all about the brewery's history and the brewing process.

BROUWERIJ TROOST

Map 2; Pazzanistraat 27, Westerpark;
///subjects.detail.narrow; www.brouwerijtroost.nl

This original branch of three Troost breweries in Amsterdam, located in Westergas's 19th-century former warehouses, is the one that locals flock to, especially if there's a glimmer of sunshine (top tip: tables at the edge of the terrace stay sunny longer). In addition to a range of classic brews and beer cocktails, there's a teetotaller-pleasing menu of home-brewed ginger beer and hoppy lemonade.

BROUWERIJ POESIAT & KATER

Map 4; Polderweg 648, Oostpoort;
///troubled.resold.pricier; www.poesiatenkater.nl

Beer-wise, you've got two ways to go at this spot: the legendary, historic Van Vollenhoven line or the modern, speciality Poesiat & Kater beers. Local Julián Álvarez is the man behind it all, brewing traditional malts to an old recipe and developing modern barley blends. Just don't let the brewery's name become a prophecy: *kater* means "hangover" (and "male cat"; *poes* is a female cat, just in case you're wondering).

OEDIPUS BREWING

Map 5; Gedempt Hamerkanaal 85, Nieuwendammerham;
///rifled.trailing.kitchens; www.oedipus.com

Everyone will tell you this taproom is worth the trek out from the centre of town as it's the only place where you'll find the full range of Oedipus beers. The on-tap offerings span pale ale, stout and grisette, designed to please local craft beer addicts. A young crowd throngs the industrial space against a backdrop of chaotic decor that takes its cues from the tropical-tinged brews.

» Don't leave without trying the flagship beer: the Mannenliefde (or "Man Love"), with hints of lemongrass and Szechuan pepper.

PENSION HOMELAND

Map 4; Kattenburgerstraat 5, Marineterrein;
///fame.bronzed.starters; www.pensionhomeland.com

The hunt for this brewery is half the fun. Your journey will take you across decommissioned naval terrain and parkland full of old marine buildings, before reaching the Homeland Hotel. Inside

Try it!
MAKE YOUR OWN BREW

Want to brew your own stout, IPA or blond? Mediamatic in Oostenburg *(www. mediamatic.net)* holds introductory workshops on beer brewing at its own MycoBrewery.

Pension, the 60s-style bar, hip Amsterdammers sip house beers (strong and leaning largely on the IPA side), served in seafarer-themed cans. If you can't get a terrace table in summer, sit on the grass to enjoy the harbour views.

DE BEKEERDE SUSTER

Map 1; Kloveniersburgwal 6, Nieuwmarkt;
///glow.bind.national; www.debekeerdesuster.nl

Once upon a time, in the 15th century, there was a convent of nuns, who took in repenting sex workers. These *bekeerde susters* (reformed nuns) spent their days brewing beer. Today a modern microbrewery inspired by these sisters stands on the same spot. Giant copper drums brew up five beers, each with their own distinct flavour, and a tasting plank lets thirsty pilgrims try them all at once, often alongside some warm, house-made beer bread. The sisters really would approve.

BROUWERIJ DE PRAEL

Map 1; Oudezijds Armsteeg 26, De Wallen;
///camp.storage.factory; www.deprael.nl

Plush brown sofas and old cabinets, just like at your grandparents' house, fill this brewpub's Tardis-like living room. The surprising amount of space is just as well: folk bands often play here, and there's even a piano on the side if you fancy striking up a tune. As for the brews? They're all additive-free and named after Dutch folk singers, of course.

Brown Pubs

Bruine Kroegen, *aka traditional pubs, are called
"brown" due to their dark wood and centuries' tobacco-
stained walls. The beating heart of locals' social lives,
they're so much more than your usual drinking den.*

CAFÉ DE DRUIF

**Map 4; Rapenburgerplein 83, Plantagebuurt;
///inhales.perform.watching; 385 23553**

Name-dropped in the letters of famous figures through history, this
kroeg is one of the oldest in the city. Everything's been left the way
your great-great-grandfather would have seen it, down to the
Turkish carpets used as tablecloths. A distillery in its former days,
Druif has a loyal fanbase of Dutch liqueur lovers.

PROEFLOKAAL DE OOIEVAAR

**Map 1; Sint Olofspoort 1, De Wallen;
///future.benched.reminds; www.proeflokaaldeooievaar.nl**

Once you set foot in Amsterdam, there's a 99 per cent chance
someone will try to teach you the word *gezellig*, an expression for a
warm and convivial atmosphere that the Dutch swear is impossible
to fully translate into another language. It's a word you'll truly

understand when you come to this *kroeg*, crammed with antique bric-a-brac. Tiny in size, big in spirit; there's no way you're getting out of here without the regulars asking you for your life story.

» **Don't leave without** trying old Amsterdam liqueurs with names such as Hemel op Aarde ("heaven on earth"). Beware, they are hugely potent. After all, in the old days they were sold here as "medicine".

HET PAPENEILAND

Map 2; Prinsengracht 2, Jordaan;
///ruler.kitchen.tree; www.papeneiland.nl

You'll see why locals call this "the Drunk Bar"; the 17th-century building leans forward like it's about to fall into the canal. Walk inside and you'll be greeted by the delicious smell of freshly baked apple pies (many will vouch these are among the best in the city). Our tip to make it even better? Pair your apple pie with a *jenever*.

IN 'T AEPJEN

Map 1; Zeedijk 15-1, De Wallen;
///outings.pound.mindset; 625 6467

Every Amsterdammer knows of In 't Aepjen. It's famous for three things: firstly, it's so old it's built of wood; secondly, it used to be a hostel for sailors returning from Dutch Indonesian colonies with their pet monkeys (weird, we know); and lastly and most importantly, it's one of the cosiest pubs in the city. There are plenty of snug corners to curl up with a hot beverage (spiked or not) when the weather doesn't play nice. Ten points for every monkey ornament you can spot.

Liked by the locals

"A *bruine kroeg* is basically the neighbourhood living room: it's the place to hear all the latest gossip, or even drop off an extra set of keys in case you get locked out of your flat (like I did)."

LINDA VAN ZANTEN, AMSTERDAM TOUR GUIDE

GOLLEM'S PROEFLOKAAL

Map 3; Overtoom 160–162, Oud-West;
///bunksrehead.aged; www.caffegollem.nl

Don't worry if you feel something brush past your legs at Gollem's; it's only the resident cat welcoming you to its home. And at home is just how you'll feel at this easy-going pub where friends enjoy quiz nights, live jazz and a mind-boggling array of beers.

CAFÉ 'T MANDJE

Map 1; Zeedijk 63, Dam; ///nods.tourist.slowly;
www.cafetmandje.amsterdam

Opened by the legendary Bet van Beeren back in 1927, this quirky spot is one of Amsterdam's most iconic queer bars. Wander in and you'll fell like you've stepped back in time: old photos are plastered on the walls and a random assortment of antiques hang from the ceiling. The vibe hasn't changed much since the early days either – it's still as fun and welcoming as ever.

PROEFLOKAAL ARENDSNEST

Map 2; Herengracht 90, Grachtengordel;
///custard.sobbed.drank; www.arendsnest.nl

It's all about the beers here. The bar staff in the cosy Eagle's Nest Tasting Room are only too happy to fill you in on the Dutch-only beer list (100 strong, with dozens on tap). Join one of the thrice-weekly tastings to tour the flavours of the Netherlands, or simply perch at the bar, tell the bartender what you like and leave your fate in their hands.

Cocktail Joints

Amsterdammers love to gather for carefully crafted cocktails and mocktails after work. Luckily, the city is peppered with cocktail bars where top mixologists invent new takes on old favourites.

BAR LABYRINTH

Map 6; Amstelveenseweg 53, Oud-Zuid;
///builds.punchy.holiday; www.labyrinthamsterdam.nl

Cocktails dusted with chocolate, infused with rosemary oil or topped with dehydrated egg foam: Samuel Kingue Ebelle's creations steal the show at his atmospheric bar. But Labyrinth isn't all about this talented mixologist's cocktails. Soul food (think fried plantain and marinated fava beans) pairs perfectly with Ebelle's drinks, while Monday open mic nights offer a dash of culture.

TALES & SPIRITS

Map 1; Lijnbaanssteeg 5–7, Grachtengordel;
///softly.smashes.insurers; www.talesandspirits.com

A long menu of quirky cocktail mixes found nowhere else? A fun and flirty waitstaff passionate about making perfect drinks with the finest spirits? An alleyway terrace that sets a new standard for charm? If this sounds like your kind of place, get to Tales & Spirits. Arrive early to claim a table, and come hungry – once you see the baskets of shared bites, you won't be able to help yourself.

» Don't leave without visiting the Tales and Spirits antique shop (open only by appointment) next door. It's full of rare vintage cocktail tools.

KEVIN BACON BAR

**Map 2; Witte de Withstraat 38, Mercatorbuurt;
///manhole.sling.talked; www.kevinbacon.nl**

Where cheeky cocktails meet Thai food, there's the cosy Kevin Bacon Bar, part of the Hotel Not Hotel. Why Kevin Bacon? Because every-body likes Kevin Bacon. Thankfully, the cocktail game here is as strong as the humour, drawing young couples and groups of friends for stunners like the Flower Power 2.0 – rose tea- infused vodka with elderflower liqueur, lavender syrup and lime elderflower tonic. And half a dozen cocktails named, of course, Kevin.

Shh!

Those not in the know easily walk past Rosalia's Menagerie *(www.rosalias.amsterdam)*, hidden in a De Wallen inn. Within its bric-a-brac-packed living room, cocktail fiends revel in the *jenever*-based fusions, true classics and seasonal inventions. If nothing takes your fancy, ask award-winning mixologist Wouter Bosch to shake you up a custom cocktail inspired by your favourite flavours.

Solo, Pair, Crowd

Hidden away in side streets and narrow alleys are plenty more bars serving top cocktails.

FLYING SOLO

Meet cute

Expect a warm welcome (and delicious cocktails) at Bar Buka, one of the city's best lesbian bars. The friendly staff will happily keep you company, but you'll find yourself chatting with the regulars in no time.

IN A PAIR

Romantic night for two

Hidden at the back of a gourmet burger joint in de Pijp, The Butcher bar is perfect for a date. Make reservations ahead to gain access to this inner sanctum, where barrel-aged concoctions await.

FOR A CROWD

Catch up with friends in style

Step away from the chaos of Leidseplein into the soothing 1950s glamour of Suzy Wong. This stylish cocktail lounge has a cool nightclub vibe, great for an evening out with friends.

VESPER BAR

Map 2; Vinkenstraat 57, Haarlemmerbuurt;
///pipeline.curvy.curl; www.vesperbar.nl

Long before the cocktail phenomenon took over the city, there was Vesper Bar. Locals in the know avoid the menu, preferring to unleash the mixologists' inner creativity by feeding them a flavour profile. (For an extra tip, of course.) Seating is limited, so keep this one to yourself.

PRIK

Map 1; Spuistraat 109, Grachtengordel;
///otters.latter.business; www.prikamsterdam.nl

Everyone is warmly welcomed at this LGBTQ+ cocktail bar. Embrace the kitsch: the space is done up like a diner in wall-to-wall pink and mixologists shake up equally colourful creations, like the Passion Swizzle – a *jenever*-based tropical fruit treat.

HIDING IN PLAIN SIGHT

Map 4; Rapenburg 18, Jodenbuurt;
///gushes.than.explains; www.hpsamsterdam.com

The artisanal cocktails have won this sultry speakeasy a cult following among locals. Sure, it's plain by design, but there's a reason that the dark, moody interior is stripped back: it's so all eyes fix on the bar, where bottles of cocktail mixers sparkle like jewels. After sampling a concoction you'll get why locals keep coming back.

» Don't leave without trying a Walking Dead, served in a crystal skull glass and set on fire.

Wine Bars

Amsterdam may be famous for beer, but its citizens are discerning wine drinkers too. Friends gather in the city's many bars over a glass of fine wine and nibbles whenever it feels like wine o'clock.

GLOU GLOU

Map 3; Tweede van der Helststraat 3, De Pijp;
///wept.suckle.trades; www.glouglou.nl

Local wine-lovers will tell you that Glou Glou, the city's original natural wine bar, is the best for those wanting to take a wine walk on the preservative-free side. There's tons of European wines to choose from, and the friendly staff happily give samples to taste before you order. The cosy space is filled with wine-sipping friends debating which is their favourite tipple while sharing charcuterie platters.

SHIRAZ

Map 3; Lijnbaansgracht 267HS, Leidseplein;
///yoga.weekday.puns; www.shirazamsterdam.nl

Middle Eastern-style hospitality meets French chic at this lovely wine bar. Tasting symbols make the menu of 150 wines easy to navigate, but the staff genuinely delight in helping you find new

Craving a little more wine knowledge? Ask about Shiraz's ever-popular wine-tasting workshops.

favourites, plus snacks to match. Want to take a bottle of your favourite wine home with you? No problem: buy it from the adjoining shop.

LILLIE WINE REBEL

Map 3; Van Breestraat 107A, Oud-Zuid; ///wishing.suckle.topples; www.lilliewinerebel.nl

Ready for an adventure? Let owner Sandra Cotiu take you on a journey to the lesser-known wine regions of the world. Shining the spotlight on grapes from the likes of Lebanon, Georgia and Greece, Cotiu's wine flights conjure up unique flavours and unforgettable stories. The wine is the main event, but don't skip the food – delicious small dishes are the perfect accompaniment.

CHATEAU AMSTERDAM

Map 5; Johan van Hasseltweg 51, Nieuwendammerham; ///rocks.slipping.talked; www.chateau.amsterdam

Once you've found out there's wine made in Amsterdam, you've got a fact even many locals don't know. This family-owned producer doesn't grow grapes locally though, it imports them from across Europe, creating unique blends and experimenting with an entire line of orange wines. Sample the lot in the tasting room and appreciate these wines made in the city for the city.

» Don't leave without taking a tour (make sure to book in advance) to get the full backstory on the wines you're sipping.

BAR GALLIZIA

Map 4; Javastraat 67, Indische Buurt;
///spin.insiders.announce; www.gallizia.nl

This is the best spot in town for Italian wines, and especially great on a sunny day (there's seating out on the pavement in front). The expert Italian and Dutch sommeliers are on hand to explain the menu's 30 by-the-glass options with a personalized tasting tour. (Go easy on them when it gets crowded.)

FABUS

Map 2; De Clercqstraat 105H, Kinkerbuurt;
///threaten.monkeys.veal; www.fabuswineandfood.com

Walk through the door of Fabus, and you'll be met with calming beige walls — a rather sedate backdrop that belies the bar's exciting menu of natural, organic and biodynamic wines. The impressive pan-European list has the city's greatest choice of Central European varieties. Peckish? The small plates on offer are equally eclectic.

» Don't leave without trying the Zweigelt, a bright-red wine made from Austria's national red grape with peppery sour cherry flavours.

RAYLEIGH & RAMSAY

Map 3; Van Woustraat 97, De Pijp; ///airship.idea.earlobe; www.rr.wine

With friends who can't agree on what bottle to order? Enter Rayleigh & Ramsay, one of Amsterdam's most popular self-service wine bars. This classy bar has a big wine selection, with 100 vintages on tap that vary in origin, taste profiles and price. On arrival you're equipped with a pre-loaded "wine card", which fills half or brimming glasses with a touch of the button. You'll find all your favourites but it's more fun to test the unknown. A word of warning: pace yourself if you want to avoid a sore head in the morning.

BUBBLES & WINES
Map 1; Nes 37, De Wallen;
///talking.bought.headline; www.bubblesandwines.com

One of the first wine bars to open in Amsterdam, Bubbles & Wines may not be as hip as its newer cousins, but it's still the city's most classically luxurious: think caviar and escargot on the bar snack menu, as well as cheese platters. As to the wine list itself – it's very well priced, nonetheless. Want to try a non-champagne bubbly? Choose from the staggering list by the glass. Fancy comparing different Bordeaux reds? Opt for one of the tasting flights (themed by wine or region) from just €12. This is where local wine lovers come for a night out when they want to feel lavish without having to splash out.

Try it!
LEARN TO MAKE WINE

Want to improve your knowledge of all things wine-related? The Amsterdam Wine Academy (www.amsterdamwineacademy. com) has enthusiasts who teach classes on wine-making and tasting.

Unmissable Terraces

It's easy to find a terrace with an awesome view in Amsterdam. At the first sign of warm sunshine, friends gather at pub and café gardens for borreltijd *by the water or surrounded by greenery.*

DE VONDELTUIN

Map 6; Vondelpark 7, Zuid; ///funny.damp.singled; www.devondeltuin.nl

For many locals, sunny weekends in the city mean one thing: long days in the Vondelpark. At its heart is a café whose large garden dares anyone to pass by without stopping – and few do. Amsterdammers from far and wide lounge on the cosy chairs, sipping local beers and fruity cocktails, while kids cavort in the adjacent playground.

» Don't leave without also checking out the Blauwe Theehuis ("Blue Teahouse") with a wraparound terrace deeper inside Vondelpark.

DAKTERRAS GAPP

Map 4; Eerste Ringdijkstraat 4, Watergraafsmeer;
///limbs.stuffing.shakes; www.hotelcasa.nl

This rooftop beer garden on the eighth floor of the Casa Hotel is an Oost icon. It opens every summer to a mixed crowd of edgy locals and cool students, who sprawl across the decking amid

There's no cover so if it rains, head down to the Casa Hotel's trendy lobby bar, with huge windows. towering plants and flower beds. There are local beers, cocktails and bar snacks aplenty, but the real draw is the endless views of the city skyline.

HANNEKES BOOM

Map 4; Dijksgracht 4, Dijkspark; ///credited.dairies.rate;
www.hannekesboom.nl

When someone asks where to meet for an after-work tipple in the city centre on a sunny day, there's really only one answer – Hannekes Boom. The huge beer garden and roof terrace of this shack-style café are packed with locals enjoying drinks with a view of the iconic Oosterdok harbour. Take a cue from those in the know and hire a boat to get here – if you can't find a seat, sip your beer from inside your moored boat while watching the sunset.

WATERKANT

Map 2; Marnixstraat 246, Jordaan; ///oddly.latches.vibrates;
www.waterkantamsterdam.nl

A waterside terrace away from the bustle of Jordaan, a laid-back vibe, craft cocktails and beers – it's no wonder that this bar is a real favourite. Groups chill out at the patio tables or lounge on floor cushions on the edge of the water, their legs dangling over the Singel canal; the banter between bar patrons and passing boaters is half the fun here. And for those after something more filling than bar snacks, the café dishes out roti rolls and other Surinamese fare.

Solo, Pair, Crowd

Sun's out? Make a go for it. Amsterdam's terraces welcome everyone, no matter what your scene is.

FLYING SOLO
Canal-side haven
For a refreshing *biertje* and a chat, grab a seat by the water at Café de Engelbewaarder in Nieuwmarkt and watch the boats go by. With its friendly staff and regulars, this place will make you feel part of the gang in no time.

IN A PAIR
Romantic garden
A crispy seafood platter for two at sunset. Gin-based cocktails. A magical setting tucked away in Westerpark. Sounds like the perfect date night? That's just what you can expect at Mossel & Gin.

FOR A CROWD
Join the party
Sit inside, on the terrace or on the beach at Pllek, the city's ultimate summer spot. There's plenty of room for the gang here, with live music, beer and campfires all on the agenda.

CAFÉ SOUNDGARDEN

Map 2; Marnixstraat 164–166, Jordaan;
///stardom.exposing.yarn; www.cafesoundgarden.nl

Rock 'n' roll lovers feel right at home in this grungy dive bar. Join the party vibe out on the waterside terrace where enthusiasts swap stories in dozens of languages to a soundtrack of great music. Want to see some local acts? Check out the packed programme.

CAFÉ DE CEUVEL

Map 5; Korte Papaverweg 2, Noord; ///uproot.doted.jiggle;
www.deceuvel.nl

This former shipyard turned social space can be anything you want it to be. Come during the day for a swim in the harbour followed by a slow afternoon sipping craft beers on the sunny terrace, or arrive in the evening for a vegan dinner followed by dancing and DJs.

» Don't leave without asking about upcoming events (previous ones have included sustainable markets and foraging workshops).

THUIS AAN DE AMSTEL

Map 6; Korte Ouderkerkerdijk 45, Amstelkwartier, Omval;
///declares.kings.rider; www.thuisaandeamstel.nl

"At Home on the Amstel" pretty much sums this place up: a café converted from an old red-brick private home, with a small gated garden that spills out onto the Amstel riverbank. It's practically a fairy tale. If inclement weather sends you retreating into the cosy inside, check out the works of art by local creatives on the walls.

Coffee Houses

The Dutch are among the world's biggest coffee drinkers so it's no surprise that the coffee house is an Amsterdam institution. Start your day, like the rest of the city, with your favourite brew.

BACK TO BLACK

Map 2; Van Hallstraat 268, Staatsliedenbuurt;
///evenly.gliding.hounded; www.backtoblackcoffee.nl

The resident cat greets coffee lovers as they enter this deliciously cosy neighbourhood spot – so tiny, in fact, that you might have to wait a bit for a seat. But it's worth it. The specialized blends here are made from carefully selected beans roasted on site. Even better, once you've discovered your favourites, you can buy some to take home.

COFFEE BRU

Map 4; Beukenplein 14, Oud-Oost;
///roofer.files.umpires; www.coffeebru.nl

Run by a trio of friendly coffee aficionados, this rustic café, filled with plants, friendly chatter and the aroma of freshly roasted beans, makes for a snug little hideout. Here you'll find students plugging away at their laptops, young families relaxing at the weekend and older folks simply relishing their afternoon espressos with a slice of freshly baked banana bread or apple pie.

SCANDINAVIAN EMBASSY
Map 3; Sarphatipark 34, De Pijp;
///rummage.onwards.possibly; www.scandinavianembassy.nl

If you're looking for the quintessential *fika* experience (the Swedish concept of spending time with friends over coffee), this is the right place. Yes, Scandinavian Embassy serves the best cinnamon buns in town, but it's the coffee that takes centre stage. The Swedish owners have scoured the roasters in Scandinavia to bring award-winning blends from home, and Amsterdammers can't get enough of it.

» Don't leave without asking about the coffee tasting sessions, where you can try unique coffee and food pairings.

LOT61 COFFEE ROASTERS
Map 2; Kinkerstraat 112, Oud-West;
///view.maker.belonging; www.lot61.com

Coffee geeks love this roastery, where Australian-born, NYC-raised owner Adam creates gourmet third-wave coffee blends. To name just two: the Bombora delivers a chocolate syrupy espresso for that early morning pre-work boost, while Nosegrind has notes of vibrant fruits that work as a post-lunch dessert. Join the regulars perching at the barrel tables and ask the staff for a recommendation – they'll know just what you need.

4850

Map 4; Camperstraat 48–50, Oud-Oost;
///twitchy.promotes.kneeled; www.4850.nl

The fresh take on Nordic-style coffee makes this sleek, Scandi spot an Oost favourite. Locals come here by day for the speciality coffees from La Cabra in Copenhagen, paired with cardamom buns. In the evening 4850 morphs into a restaurant, so why not stay on for dinner rounded off by a delicious single-origin coffee.

BARMHARTIG KOFFIE

Map 4; Veemkade 1228, Oostelijk Havengebied;
///fund.handy.urge; www.barmhartigkoffie.nl

Hidden away above a corner supermarket, this coffee house is easy to miss. But walk up the stairs and you'll find a surprisingly roomy space with large windows overlooking the Eastern Docklands (regulars bag the window seats, so get here early to beat them to it). Barmhartig Koffie is more than just coffee heaven with a view though; it doubles as a salon a few days each week.

THE COFFEE VIRUS

Map 5; Overhoeksplein 2, Overhoeks;
///booklet.fondest.meals; www.thecoffeevirus.nl

Ideally positioned inside the Amsterdam University of Arts' Breitner Academy building, and around the corner from the Eye Filmmuseum *(p125)*, this cool-kid coffee house is a favourite among the city's arty students. Join them here as they discuss their favourite movies and recent art exhibitions over endless cups of coffee. Bring your laptop or journal, too — it's the kind of place where you're sure to be inspired.

COFFEE & COCONUTS
Map 3; Ceintuurbaan 282–284, De Pijp;
///resold.inviting.raced; www.coffeeandcoconuts.com

Most Amsterdammers agree that there are few more beautiful cafés in the city than this Art Deco cinema-turned-holiday-vibes coffee spot. Picnic tables are dotted under the cathedral-high ceiling, vintage black-and-white photos and leafy plants adorn the brick walls and large beanbags in the loft seat stylish locals. And the coffee? The roastery uses quality beans from all over the world. It's the perfect place to hang out with a gaggle of friends on a lazy Sunday afternoon.

» Don't leave without pairing your coffee with pancakes, drenched in silky coconut cream, with a sprinkle of toasted coconut flakes (this place is just as much about the nut as about coffee, after all).

Try it!
SPILL THE BEANS

Fancy tasting some coffees? The Starbucks Concept Store in Rembrandtplein is where new coffees are tested for the entire European market. Have your say at one of the regular cupping (that's tasting) sessions.

0 metres 500
0 yards 500

Get in the spirit at
DE DRIE FLESCHJES

Sip on a *jenever*, paired with hearty
meatballs or sausages, at this 1650s bar.
Don't miss the quirky collection of small
bottles with hand-painted portraits of
Amsterdam's former mayors.

The Gin Festival at
Beurs van Berlage *(an*
events and exhibitions
space), held around
mid-May, runs tastings
and workshops.

WESTER-
MARKT

3

DAMRAK

CENTRUM

DAM

GRACHTEN-
GORDEL

2

Singel

NIEUWE
ZIJDE

Snoop around
WYNAND FOCKINK

You'll hear all about the
17th-century methods of
making *jenever* and liqueurs at
this *proeflokaal* (tasting room
and bar). It's Amsterdam's
oldest, in business since 1679.

Proeflokaal A van
Wees *was one of*
Amsterdam's oldest
distilleries. It's now a
pub, with 60 brands of
Dutch liqueurs.

O.VOORBURGWAL

WATERLOO
PLEIN

ROKIN

Amstel

Herengracht

MUNT-
PLEIN

REMBRANDT-
PLEIN

Keizersgracht

VIJZELSTR

NASSAUKADE

Prinsengracht

NIEUWE
SPIEGELSTR

UTRECHTSESTRAAT

LEIDSE-
PLEIN

SPIEGELGR

1

MUSEUM-
PLEIN

STADHOUDERSKADE

Discover the secret at
HOUSE OF BOLS

Immerse yourself in the interactive Cocktail and
Jenever Experience at this distillery and museum
to find out more about *jenever*. You can create
your perfect cocktail (including non-alcoholic
varieties) at the do-it-yourself bar.

OUD-
ZUID

ZUID

Sarphatipark

DE PIJP

An afternoon sampling
Dutch spirits

Jenever, a juniper-flavoured liqueur and close relation of gin, has been made in the Netherlands for hundreds of years. In fact, the term "Dutch courage" comes from soldiers drinking *jenever* before battle back in the day. Mercifully, enjoying *jenever* is a much more civilized affair these days; brown pubs and cool cocktail bars serve it in small tulip-shaped glasses, filled to the brim (you'll need to bow your head to take your first sip). Swot up on *jenever*'s history and production in the Netherlands and sample some of Amsterdam's finest spirits on this tour.

1. House of Bols
Paulus Potterstraat 12–16,
Oud-Zuid; www.bols.com
///feels.opposite.alleges

2. Wynand Fockink
Pijlsteeg 31, Oude Centrum;
www.wynand-fockink.nl
///jacket.diet.yarn

3. De Drie Fleschjes
Gravenstraat 81,
Oude Centrum; www.
dedriefleschjes.nl
///vets.munched.alright

Beurs van Berlage
///fees.deserved.refuse

Proeflokaal A van Wees
///breezes.serve.cattle

85

SHOP

Forget generic high street stores: Amsterdammers love nothing more than celebrating local designers, scouting vintage gems and indulging in organic produce.

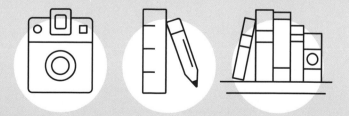

Street Markets

Amsterdam's street markets epitomize the locals'
obsession with all things fresh, vintage and unique.
Almost every neighbourhood has its own market,
teeming with bargain and treasure hunters.

TEN KATEMARKT

Map 2; Ten Katestraat 34, Kinkerbuurt;
///vampire.milder.bronzed; www.tenkatemarkt.nl

Sure, there are many international street food stalls at De Foodhallen
(p56), just around the corner from here, but locals prefer to come to
Ten Katemarkt. Why? The vibe's more laid back, the prices are lower
and most of the food trucks are family-run. Pick up an Italian deli-
style sandwich or steaming Nepali momo dumplings, then wash
them down with bubble tea. A true foodie haven.

ALBERT CUYPMARKT

Map 3; Albert Cuypstraat, De Pijp; ///clinked.husbands.grinning;
www.albertcuyp-markt.amsterdam

Ask any Amsterdammer where to try the best Dutch street snacks
and they'll direct you to Albert Cuypmarkt. Warm *stroopwafels*,
poffertjes (mini-pancakes) and *friet* (chips) are served up amid a

Around the corner from Albert Cuypmarkt is Katsu Coffeeshop, which serves hot drinks and quality cannabis.

cacophany of merchants loudly touting their cheeses, fruit and veg, herbs, spices, second-hand clothes and flowers. Expect queues, but the food is worth the wait.

DAPPERMARKT

Map 4; Dapperstraat 279, Dapperbuurt;
///season.briefer.pool; www.dappermarkt.nl

Few tourists make it to Dappermarkt, which is exactly why you should venture here. Running for more than 100 years, it's a glorious celebration of cultures. People chatter away in numerous languages, with many families gathering simply to socialize. As for the goods, you'll find bargain-priced speciality groceries, quality Indian fabrics, Moroccan aromatic spices and the best kebabs in the city (no really, they're unbeatable).

WATERLOOPLEINMARKT

Map 4; Waterlooplein 2, Nieuwmarkt;
///magical.guides.modules; www.waterlooplein.amsterdam

The city's oldest flea market is a dream for lovers of all things vintage and handmade. Bargain-hunting hippies rummage through clothes and records; students skim through old books and steampunk gadgets; hipsters buy spare parts for their bikes and funky hand-knitted jumpers. Bring a couple of tote bags – you'll need them.

» Don't leave without trying a giant *loempia* (spring roll) from the Vietnamese food truck. If the owner is in a good mood, she'll sing to you.

IJ-HALLEN

Map 5; TT Neveritaweg 15, NDSM;
///jaunts.brush.pitchers; www.ijhallen.nl

Fancy an antique camera to capture your next weekend away?
Or some second-hand garms for your big night out? This enormous
monthly flea market in two industrial warehouses will have whatever
you're after. It's the biggest of its kind in Europe, after all. That said,
this is very much a community space, where commercial vendors
are swapped out for families and flatmates selling their personal
treasures. You'll lose all sense of time searching among the heaps
of goods, surrounded by the echoes of haggling Amsterdammers.

NOORDERMARKT

Map 2; Noordermarkt 48, Jordaan;
///stole.define.classic; www.noordermarkt-amsterdam.nl

The Noordermarkt started out as a pottery market in the 17th
century, selling the beloved Chinese-inspired Delftware that the
Netherlands is famous for. Nowadays, the Monday morning market
is where you'll still find ceramics (and at reasonable prices, too), but
it's just as much about paintings and vintage clothing.

NIEUWMARKT

Map 1; Nieuwmarkt; ///feed.remarked.walks

This is Amsterdam just as it used to be: fishmongers shout out the
catch of the day and farmers chat away with couples stocking up
on veggies for their evening meal. Visit on a Saturday for organic

produce, artisan bread and flowers. All day on summer Sundays, antiques vendors take over the square with bric-a-brac, vintage clothes and new designer toys, satisfying your shopping needs late into the weekend.

» Don't leave without stepping inside the 1488 De Waag, originally a city gate and now a restaurant with a bar and generous terrace.

WESTERGAS SUNDAY MARKET
Map 2; Pazzanistraat 33, Westerpark;
///vanish.composer.noses; www.sundaymarket.nl

On the first Sunday of every month Amsterdam's designers and artists set up stalls in Westergas, an industrial-turned-creative complex inside Westerpark. Young families and curio hunters browse the handmade ceramics, housewares, clothes and jewellery to a backdrop of live music, stopping for snacks at the organic cafés as they go. If you love fashion, art and street food, this is the market for you.

DE BOEKENMARKT OP HET SPUI
Map 1; Spui; ///brothers.nuance.engages;
www.deboekenmarktophetspui.nl

Every book-loving Amsterdammer raves about this used book market, which sees friendly booksellers from all over the Netherlands gather in the city centre every Friday. There are literally hundreds of tomes to flick through, covering just about every subject in multiple languages. A word of warning: you're bound to come away with a hefty reading list.

Dutch Design

The Netherlands and its capital have long been a hub for creativity, born out of the risk-taking that comes with a city built below sea level. These favourite stores showcase just some of the city's creations.

VELORETTI

Map 3; Van Woustraat 72, De Pijp;
///match.fracture.sculpture; www.veloretti.com

Inspired by this bike obsessed city? Head over to Veloretti's light-filled brandstore to browse some stylish two-wheelers. Designed in Amsterdam and handmade in Europe, these bikes come in a

Shh!

Spiegel *(www.spiegelamsterdam. nl)* is a lovely little gift shop in the centre of the city. A quieter alternative to the bustling I Amsterdam Store *(p95)*, Spiegel offers 100 per cent Dutch designed products that make gorgeous presents and keepsakes. Trinkets, table-ware and toys are all on offer, including Miffy, the cute fictional rabbit created by Dutch artist Dick Bruna. Swing by for the perfect souvenir.

gorgeous array of muted tones, with electric options available too. Not sure which model is best for you? The in-house experts really know their stuff and are on hand to answer any questions.

MOOOI AMSTERDAM BRAND STORE

Map 2; Westerstraat 187, Jordaan; ///respect.voted.gosh; www.moooi.com
Moooi (the Dutch word for "beautiful") more than lives up to the standards of owner Marcel Wanders, one of the Netherlands' best-loved designers. Bold and edgy, this gigantic new-age design store in the Jordaan (a neighbourhood where many a home is decked out in kooky Moooi interiors) resembles an avant-garde art museum more than a home furnishings shop. Wander around the lamps that resemble trees and clocks assembled from origami birds and you'll soon feel like Alice in Wonderland.

THE MAKER STORE

Map 2; Hannie Dankbaarpassage 39, Oud-West;
///breathed.device.follow; www.themakerstore.nl
The Maker Store is the kind of place where you come in look-ing for a birthday gift for your pal and end up leaving with tote bags stuffed with things for yourself. And why are we always surprised? This place curates lovingly crafted items (like funky mugs and scented candles) from more than 90 local brands. Come prepared to spend, you've been warned.

» Don't leave without asking about The Maker Market that takes place just outside the store once a month.

UNITED NUDE

Map 1; Molsteeg 10, Spuistraat, Oude Centrum;
///triangle.salt.piglet; www.unitednude.com

If you were wondering where young Amsterdammers get their
chunky trainers and cube-heeled sandals, this is the place. The
creative mind behind the innovative footwear brand is the
architecturally trained designer, Rem D Koolhaas. Every pair
of shoes is a reinterpretation of an architectural object: like the
"Möbius" shoe, inspired by the iconic Barcelona chair.

DROOG

Map 1; Staalstraat 7B, Plantagebuurt;
///elite.exposes.cardinal; www.droog.com

Droog means "dry" in Dutch, but this fun design store, which works
with top designers like Marcel Wanders and Hella Jongerious, is
anything but – think bright milk bottle lamps, hare-shaped door mats
and the top half of a teapot for one. There's also an equally quirky
café and exhibition space, which has Dali-esque art installations and
overlooks a fairy-tale landscaped garden. Dreamy stuff.

ATELIER MUNRO

Map 3; Beethovenstraat 19, Oud-Zuid;
///riders.spend.singles; www.ateliermunro.com

Not all suits are cut from the same cloth, and neither is their maker.
That's the ethos of Atelier Munro, a bespoke Amsterdam menswear
company that prides itself on creating custom-made clothing.

Appointments to create your fit profile are free, and you'll learn what flatters your specific body type.

Modern sartorialists will find anything from suits to jeans, ties to shoes, at a range of price points. Choose at the store and order online from home.

I AMSTERDAM STORE

Map 5; De Ruijterkade 28B, Centraal Station; ///fracture.fanfare.slot;
www.iamsterdam.com/nl/i-amsterdam-store

You could easily walk past the I Amsterdam Store in the city's busy Centraal Station without any clue that some of the best Dutch designs can be found here. Much more than just a tourist info point, it's where locals shop for hand-picked, unique Amsterdam-made gifts and home accessories from Dutch designers. There's nothing touristy about these products, though they do cost a pretty penny.

LOCALS

Map 1; Spuistraat 272, Oude Centrum;
///animate.item.plenty; www.localsamsterdam.com

Clothing, accessories, home decor and more – this concept shop showcases sustainably minded Dutch designers of all stripes. Looking for some fashion-forward, colourfully casual clothing like you've seen worn on Amsterdam's streets? This is your spot. Artist, designer and owner Suzanne Hof is all too happy to help you put together that perfect Dutch-designed outfit once you walk through the door. Ask her about Sugarz, her line of colourful stone jewellery, sold here too.

Gourmet Treats

*When it comes to seeking out gourmet gifts or
ingredients for a special meal, these are just some of the
shops that Amsterdammers frequent. You too can snap
up treats to take home or enjoy on a canal-side picnic.*

TONY'S CHOCOLONELY SUPERSTORE

**Map 1; Oudebrugsteeg 15, Dam; ///display.hedge.amount;
www.tonyschocolonely.com**

If Willy Wonka were to go chocolate shopping in Amsterdam, he'd
head to Tony's, where friendly staff invite you to sample all kinds of
chocolate flavours amid topsy-turvy furniture – you can even create
your own bar. The chocolates taste good, and the ethical Dutch
brand does good, too: Tony's works directly with cocoa farmers in
West Africa to fight child labour and modern slavery.

LITTLE PLANT PANTRY

**Map 3; Bosboom Toussaintstraat 45H, Oud-West;
///breezes.grass.secrets; www.littleplantpantry.com**

Plastic-free wholefoods stores were nowhere to be found in
Amsterdam until Maria and Winter moved here from Ireland to set
this place up. The zero-waste, healthy approach was a hit, thanks to

plant-based delicacies that herbivores, eco-warriors and even meat-eaters rave about. Shelves burst with cheeses, homemade kimchi and organic quinoa, while the food service counter at the back promises comfort food like your granny makes; expect nutritious soups, vegetable stews and pies perfect for a chilly day.

DE BIERKONING

Map 1; Paleisstraat 125, Dam; ///twigs.tonsils.drifter; www.bierkoning.nl

Reverence is wholly encouraged at this emporium, lovingly referred to as the "Beer King of Amsterdam". For beer lovers there's few greater joys than crossing the threshold and gazing upon the glorious sight of 2,000 beers. It may be small, but every inch of space is utilized: local beers share space with varieties from all around the world, including craft beers you'll be hard-pressed to find anywhere else. Cheers to that.

» Don't leave without asking one of the staff to help you put together your ideal selection of craft beers to impress your friends.

Shh!

If you're in the market for something a little stronger than beer, keep an eye out for Dutch spirits store Slijterij De Vreng & Zonen *(75 Nieuwendijk)*, hidden around the corner from De Bierkoning. This antiquey spot surprises with unique wares, including absinthe and gin in bottles shaped like machine guns and motorbikes. P.S. Check out the website to discover a range of cocktail recipes – handy for experimenting with your new purchase.

ALBERT HEIJN

Map 3; Van Baerlestraat 33a, Oud-Zuid;
///glitter.learns.tonsils; www.ah.nl

If you want to take home some tasty *stroopwafels* to share with your family and work pals, there's nowhere better to shop for them than at Amsterdam's most ubiquitous chain of supermarkets. Wait, what? It's true. Albert Heijn stocks the full range of flavours (traditional caramel, sure, but what about honey, chocolate or mango-chilli?), and there's no tourist mark-up either. Oh, and while you're here, take a look at the other Dutch biscuits too. After all, no one is ever disappointed by more sweet treats.

FROMAGERIE ABRAHAM

Map 5; Van der Pekplein 1b, Noord; ///glorious.invest.bend;
www.abrahamkef.nl

Locals often cycle to this cheese shop to stock up on Dutch and French delights for their next dinner party. The strong among them cycle home after, but the weak (of will)? Well, you'll find them sitting outside the

Try it!
MAKE GOUDA

Fancy learning how to make cheese? Simonehoeve *(www.simonehoeve.com),* a cheese farm and clog factory 15 km (9 miles) outside Amsterdam, offers Gouda-making workshops.

Luckily for cheese-lovers not in Noord, Fromagerie Abraham have locations in Oost and the centre, too.

shop's restaurant (Proeflokaal Kef), glass of wine in hand and platter of cheese before them. Because when the cheese is this good, it's hard to resist trying it on the spot.

HARAR COFFEE

Map 2;Tweede Hugo de Grootstraat 22, Jordaan;
///cheerful.awards.scout; www.hararcoffee.nl

Having grown up among the coffee plantations of Ethiopia, Harar Coffee owner Masho learned exactly what makes a great brew from a young age. And though she now lives in Amsterdam, Masho travels home regularly to source and bring back coffee that's not only organic and single origin but also fair trade (a concept coined in the Netherlands, don't you know). Follow the lead of coffee connoisseurs by paying her a visit and picking up some beans – the perfect accompaniment to the weekend newspaper.

CASA DEL GUSTO

Map 3; Kerkstraat 121, Grachtengordel;
///prone.certified.format; 330 8330

Italian Amsterdammers head to this deli to stock up on special ingredients from home: pastas (wheat, egg and gluten-free), risotto rice, fine cheeses, olive oils and lemonade, to name but a few. Owners Gessica and Gianni love sharing their expert knowledge of the produce, which they get directly from small suppliers and farms in Tuscany and Umbria.

>> Don't leave without picking up a juicy ciabatta sandwich, filled with your choice of cheese and ham, spinach and peppers.

Vintage Stores

Amsterdammers love mixing the old with the new. Amped up on the thrill of the hunt to find something unique, they indulge their passion for fashion, history and sustainability at these fine vintage stores.

WE ARE VINTAGE

Map 2; Kinkerstraat 193, Kinkerbuurt; ///steadily.splash.forever; www.rumorsvintage.nl

It's all about the 60s vibes at this eclectic store, a favourite among local fashionistas and hipsters. Join them scouring the fringe vests, go-go boots and rainbow-coloured crochet ponchos that line the shelves, and (if you're feeling bold), sashaying down the store's makeshift runway. Time here is time well spent, if you ask us.

ZIPPER

Map 2; Huidenstraat 7, Negen Straatjes, Grachtengordel; ///list.beats.language; www.zippervintageclothing.com

Run by an American couple and their son, Zipper is a time capsule of 20th-century USA. Quality Chicago Bulls jerseys, Cooper flight jackets and cosy knits fill the two narrow floors of one of Amsterdam's oldest vintage stores, and there's even a rack

Learn more about sustainable fashion at the Fashion for Good museum, a five-minute walk away.

dedicated to a true Dutch necessity: waterproof raincoats. Zipper also recycles clothing to create new garments under the house label Ultra Zipper.

BIS!

Map 1; Sint Antoniesbreestraat 25A, Nieuwmarkt;
///quiz.notebook.motivate; www.bis-vintage.nl

Grandma's attic meets grandad's military trunk at Bis!, which has earned true celeb status among Amsterdammers. Cool kids rifle through the colossal collection of army and navy classics for the military look. Dapper folk are drawn to the suits and dashing hats. Jazz Age-loving locals scout for polka-dot frocks and scarves to complete their sassy look. Whatever time period or part of the world you're looking to travel to sartorially, you'll almost certainly find what you're looking for here.

KILO STORE

Map 4; Jodenbreestraat 158, Plantagebuurt;
///backward.sporting.typist; www.kiloshop.nl

The concept at this vintage gem is simple: choose it, weigh it, pay for it. Here, clothes and accessories are organized by colour and weight into neat shelves and shipshape displays. After a bargain leather jacket for autumn? Want to jump on the 90s athleisure bandwagon? Looking for a bag for that special occasion? Tick, tick and double-tick: Kilo Store has got you covered.

Liked by the locals

"The Dutch are often called cheapskates, but I'm proud of this. Vintage shops are my weakness – not just because of the money I'm saving, but because I can minimize contributing to environmental pollution."

MYRTE JANSOPHAR, A BORN-AND-BRED
AMSTERDAMMER

OLD WEST

Map 2; De Clercqstraat 63, Oud-West;
///sugars.forms.broads; www.oldwestamsterdam.nl

Passionate about recycling quality clothes, two friends founded this second-hand children's store, now beloved by young parents and their little ones. Because second-hand doesn't mean second-best, there are plenty of pieces in mint condition from top brand names.

» Don't leave without trading in some of your kids' used clothes in exchange for shop credit. You'll want to come back, trust us.

EPISODE

Map 4; Waterlooplein 1, Nieuwmarkt;
///removed.drank.desks; www.episode.eu

There's more to this shop than meets the eye. Episode carefully selects one-off pieces from sorting companies, repairs and then washes them in energy-saving machines powered by its very own solar panels. And despite being the biggest vintage chain in the Netherlands, it continues to stick to its principles of sustainability.

LAURA DOLS

Map 2; Wolvenstraat 7, Grachtengordel;
///impose.vocally.seagull; www.lauradols.nl

Style-conscious Amsterdammers head to Laura Dols for truly show-stopping outfits. Beaded 1920s gowns paired with long satin gloves, 30s tuxedos and top hats, and 50s cocktail dresses and matching handbags hark back to the Golden Age of Hollywood glamour.

Book Nooks

Ever since its key role in the European printing industry back in the 17th century, Amsterdam has been the bookshop of the world. Find your next read at one of these local favourites.

BOEKHANDEL PERDU

**Map 1; Kloveniersburgwal 86, De Wallen;
///fattest.colonies.certainty; www. perdu.nl/en/boekhandel**

Perdu lives and breathes poetry. This little book shop is packed with Dutch and International verse, but it doesn't stop at selling. A full roster of events give practising poets a voice in Amsterdam's arty community. Look out for book presentations, writing workshops and open mic events, many of which are hosted in the shop's secret theatre.

Try it!
PEN YOUR OWN BOOK

Always thought about writing your own novel? Amsterdam Writing Workshops *(www.amsterdamwriting.com)* offers creative writing classes for aspiring and established authors in the English language.

ATHENAEUM BOEKHANDEL
Map 1; Spui 14–16; ///fence.vehicle.started;
www.athenaeum.nl

You'll spot this gem of a shop by its retro red-and-white awnings. Inside, curvy stairways lead to different mezzanines and hidden reading corners where dishevelled literati browse the best in languages, philosophy and science publications; it's easy to lose sight of your friends between the never-ending rows of literary classics and academic tomes. Not that it's all scholarly volumes, mind – Athenaeum also has the best range of lifestyle, indie and any other type of magazines in the city. You'll feel smarter just wandering the warrens of this encyclopedic bookshop.

AMERICAN BOOK CENTER
Map 1; Spui 12; ///trainer.deflect.remarked; www.abc.nl

Smack in the middle of Spui, this mammoth bookshop may resemble a chain store, but it's anything but. The independent, family-owned bookshop has held a special place in locals' hearts since 1972, a sanctuary for like-minded readers who find comfort in the sheer volume of tomes. Don't know where to start? Browse the store's centrepiece: a lofty spiral staircase, where recommended books marked "ABC favourites" line the wall from floor to ceiling. And if all that reading has got you inspired, head to Betty the Book Machine on the second floor to self-publish the book you've been penning at an affordable price.

» Don't leave without signing up for one of the regular book launches or author talks popular with the local book-loving community.

THE BOOK EXCHANGE

Map 1; Kloveniersburgwal 58, De Wallen;
///coaching.inclined.pitching; www.bookexchange.nl

Rickety wooden flooring, wonky shelves and low ceilings make this old-school bookshop the perfect, snug hideaway from the mayhem of De Wallen. Second-hand English books of all genres densely line the walls, so whether you're after popular pulp crime fiction, a classic novel, poetry or a scholarly tome, there's bound to be something here for you. The cheery staff are more than happy to help you find what you're looking for.

HENK COMICS & MANGA STORE

Map 1; Zeedijk 101C, De Wallen; ///torches.evolving.visits; www.comics.nl

Behind a narrow storefront, Henk is every comic book fan's utopia. Endless shelves are crammed with new and second-hand graphic novels, comics and manga, and cabinets burst with figurines. It also hosts events; the Batman and Halloween parties are favourites.

Shh!

Oudemanhuispoort is a covered passage, lined with gorgeous historical buildings that are part of Amsterdam University. It hosts a daily second-hand book market where booksellers offer a myriad of classics, contemporary reads, old prints and vintage posters.

HAPPY BOOKIEMAN

Map 1; Herengracht 267A, Grachtengordel;
///senior.deflate.usages; 447 21114

Welcome to the cosy front room of Steve's old canal-side house (yes, this is literally his home), where anyone is invited to browse the books freely. It's dark and disorganized, with random second-hand books of all genres flying off the shelves and piles of hardbacks lying on the floor among the bric-a-brac, but that's all part of its quirky charm (as are the rock-bottom prices). In balmy summer months, feel free to bring a beer, pick a book and sit at the small table out front, where Steve might just join you.

SCHELTEMA

Map 1; Rokin 9, De Wallen;
///spin.crawler.bothered; www.scheltema.nl

Sprawling across five levels and stocked with more than 120,000 books, Scheltema is the country's largest (and arguably most iconic) bookstore. A much-loved Amsterdam institution, it's been standing on the Rokin since 1853. Families with little ones flock to the whimsical kids' section; literature lovers browse the endless shelves of novels (in multiple languages); students veer towards the secret collection of second-hand books tucked away on the top floor. There's also a huge selection of vintage globes, maps and travel books, a dream-come-true for those with wanderlust. And for folks wanting a coffee break, there's Vascobelo on the first floor, the only café in an Amsterdam bookstore. You could easily while away a whole afternoon here.

A morning of
vintage shopping

On the hunt for unique treasures from yesteryear? Join gaggles of magpie-eyed Amsterdammers and make for the Spiegelkwartier (literally the "mirror quarter"), the heart of the city's art and antiques trade for more than 80 years. This pretty patch is lined with 17th-century narrow town houses that form the perfect setting for the 70 specialized shops selling pre-loved vinyl, clothing, pottery and curiosities.

1. Droomfabriek de Groot & de Jong
Nieuwe Spiegelstraat 9B, Spiegelkwartier;
www.droomfabriekantiek.nl
///drop.enable.journals

2. Episode
Nieuwe Spiegelstraat 37H, Spiegelkwartier;
www.episode.eu
///conveys.turkeys.hosts

3. Kramer Kunst & Antiek
Prinsengracht 807, Spiegelkwartier;
www.antique-tileshop.nl
///money.beefed.ticket

4. Record Palace Weteringschans
Weteringschans 33A, Spiegelkwartier;
www.recordstoreday.nl
///minus.finishes.robots

📍 **Museum Van Loon**
///already.hands.blanked

📍 **De Stedemaagd**
///composer.part.petal

De Stedemaagd
(or *The City Maid*) sits over the entrance to Vondelpark, her right hand inviting shoppers and walkers to enter.

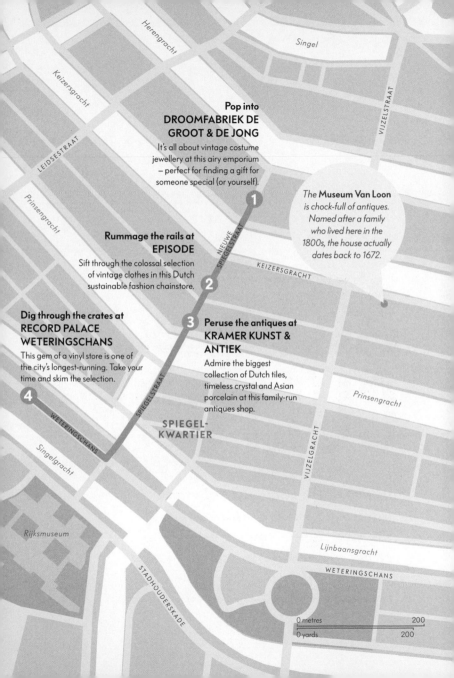

**Pop into
DROOMFABRIEK DE
GROOT & DE JONG**

It's all about vintage costume
jewellery at this airy emporium
– perfect for finding a gift for
someone special (or yourself).

1

*The Museum Van Loon
is chock-full of antiques.
Named after a family
who lived here in the
1800s, the house actually
dates back to 1672.*

**Rummage the rails at
EPISODE**

Sift through the colossal selection
of vintage clothes in this Dutch
sustainable fashion chainstore.

2

3

**Dig through the crates at
RECORD PALACE
WETERINGSCHANS**

This gem of a vinyl store is one of
the city's longest-running. Take your
time and skim the selection.

4

**Peruse the antiques at
KRAMER KUNST &
ANTIEK**

Admire the biggest
collection of Dutch tiles,
timeless crystal and Asian
porcelain at this family-run
antiques shop.

SPIEGEL-
KWARTIER

0 metres 200
0 yards 200

ARTS & CULTURE

Amsterdam is a cultural giant. Museums tell the vital stories of the past, while small galleries and street murals comment on the present and future.

City History

*The Netherlands and its capital have been shaped
by trade and immigration, made possible by the city's
waterways. Learn all about it – and so much more –
at these museums and on insightful tours.*

AMSTERDAM MUSEUM
Map 4; H'ART, Amstel 51, Plantagebuurt;
///linen.level.pebble; www.amsterdammuseum.nl

Everyone knows Amsterdam as the home of Rembrandt and the Red
Light District, but that's not all that marks this city's history. This fascinating museum (housed in H'ART Museum until 2027) takes a
deep dive into Amsterdam's story, with exhibits on the Gay Games of
1998, Ajax football fandom and female experiences of the city.

TROPENMUSEUM
Map 4; Linnaeusstraat 2, Oud-Oost;
///gates.blazing.nails; www.tropenmuseum.nl

Amsterdam is a city of world cultures, and this oft-overlooked spot
is dedicated to the connections between people across the globe.
Housed in the former Dutch Colonial Institute, the Museum of the
Tropics not only shows the huge diversity of the Netherlands, but

also tackles the country's colonial history. Exhibitions sensitively depict stories of the past, present and future, whether it's a video on the legacies of slavery or an artwork reflecting on the crisis in Syria.

JEWISH HISTORICAL MUSEUM

Map 4; Nieuwe Amstelstraat 1, Plantagebuurt;
///straws.ships.parties; www.jck.nl

Ever since Jewish merchants began to settle in Amsterdam from the late 16th century, the city has been home to one of Europe's liveliest Jewish populations. And this museum is a space for that community to learn about their Dutch Jewish identity. Though the permanent collection of artifacts is great, it's the temporary exhibitions and film screenings that really draw inquisitive minds. Oh, and the Hebrew and music lessons that keep the kids entertained.

>> Don't leave without planning a visit to the Anne Frankhuis and the National Holocaust Museum (due to open in 2024) to learn more about the Nazi persecution of the Jewish community in World War II.

GRACHTENMUSEUM

Map 2; Herengracht 386, Grachtengordel;
///giggles.status.lure; www.grachten.museum

Amsterdam's 165 canals aren't all about scenic views – they have a history, too, and the Museum of the Canals shares it. Holograms, videos and models show how the Grachtengordel (canal belt) was built to accommodate the increasing number of immigrants in the 17th century, and explain the role of waterways in the city's history.

RED LIGHT SECRETS: MUSEUM OF PROSTITUTION

**Map 1; Oudezijds Achterburgwal 60, Ouderkerksplein,
De Wallen; ///rigid.tiling.lion; www.redlightsecrets.com**

The Red Light District, bathed in a red neon glow, is one of the defining images of Amsterdam. De Wallen, as it's known to the locals, is a controversial part of the city, and that's exactly why a mind-opening visit to the world's only prostitution museum is a must. At this former brothel, the history of the industry and the dangers that sex workers face daily are explored in a respectful and empathetic way. One minute, you're sitting on a high stool behind a screen that projects passersby; the next, you're learning about the measures taken to prevent sex trafficking and listening to clips that narrate personal stories and secrets. Expect to leave with new perspectives.

» Don't leave without booking yourself onto a tour run by the Prostitution Information Centre. Former sex workers lead walk-and-talk sessions about the social conditions of sex workers.

LGBTQ+ HISTORY TOUR

**Map 2; Special Amsterdam Tours, Homomonument, Westermarkt,
Grachtengordel; ///shunts.shady.crawled; www.specialamsterdamtours.nl**

This is a city that delights in difference, so it's no surprise that it was the gay capital of the world in the 1980s and 90s. You'll be hard-pressed to find someone who knows Amsterdam's LGBTQ+ landscape like lively historian Henk, who uncovers the city's long history of queer activism and culture on this walking tour. From the Homomonument – the world's first monument commemorating

Head to the OBA Library in Oosterdok, where you'll find the biggest LGBTQ+ archive in Europe.

those who've been persecuted for their sexual orientation – Henk leads you to LGBTQ+ landmarks, ending at Café de 't Mandje, one of the city's oldest gay bars.

VERZETSMUSEUM

Map 4; Plantage Kerklaan 61, Plantagebuurt;
///brighter.cube.pursuit; www.verzetsmuseum.org

Amsterdammers are a courageous bunch, and nowhere exemplifies this quite like the Dutch Resistance Museum. Reconstructed streets, photographs and personal items uncover what life was like during the Nazi occupation of Amsterdam in World War II, and how the underground Dutch resistance movement fought back. Powerful stuff.

BLACK HERITAGE AND COLONIAL HISTORY TOUR

Map 1; Damstraat 3, Dam;
///settle.formal.teachers; www.blackheritagetours.com

Any local who has taken this thought-provoking boat tour never views the city's historical sights in the same way again – and that's the whole point. Through heartfelt stories about the African diaspora, Surinamese-American author Jennifer Tosch sheds light on the little-known and often unspoken history of people of colour in Amsterdam, as well as the uncomfortable truths that lie behind the gabled mansions and old museums built during the 17th-century. It's a hidden history that deserves the limelight.

Art & Photography

Vermeer, Frans Hals, Van Gogh. Yes you'll find them all here, but this is a city that looks forward as much as it does back. Discover the next Rembrandt in one of the many thought-provoking art museums.

NXT MUSEUM

Map 5; Asterweg 22, Overhoeks, Noord;
///belonging.include.bangle; www.nxtmuseum.com

Okay, Amsterdam may not be the next Silicon Valley, but it's quite the tech-loving city. Warmly welcomed on its opening in 2020, this new media gallery encourages pioneering artists to open local minds through a mash-up of art and technology. Expect immersive exhibits that tackle all the important topics, like whether AI is threatening civil rights or if surveillance is going too far.

FOAM PHOTOGRAPHY MUSEUM

Map 3; Keizersgracht 609, Grachtengordel;
///puts.kitten.pushed; www.foam.org

Amsterdammers are pretty into their photography – unsurprising given how photogenic the city is. This spot keeps that passion alive, showcasing new talents who tackle bold subject matters like drug

In town in spring? Don't miss the World Press Photo show that starts in Amsterdam before touring the world.

addiction or refugee stories. Those who dream of seeing their own work on the walls here one day can be found at weekend workshops and evening talks.

RIJKSMUSEUM

Map 3; Museumstraat 1, Museumplein, Oud-Zuid;
///beefed.udder.podcast; www.rijksmuseum.nl

You know a museum means business when the locals refer to it as the "Museum of the Kingdom". You'd be forgiven for letting the 8,000-strong collection and unbearably long queues overwhelm you, but persevere: beyond the crowds gathering around the 17th century paintings and Asian pavilion are special exhibitions, weekend workshops, and even cocktail and jazz nights on a Friday.

HET REMBRANDTHUIS

Map 4; Jodenbreestraat 4, Plantagebuurt;
///ample.openings.kick; www.rembrandthuis.nl

Fair warning: you're not going to find Rembrandt's biggest masterpieces here; head to the Rijksmuseum for that. You're in for something even better: a tour of Rembrandt's life in the house where Amsterdam's most beloved artist spent his best years. Discover how his financial scandals ruined him, see his studio and gawp at his etchings.

» Don't leave without watching a demonstration of how Rembrandt and his apprentices used to mix their paints.

Solo, Pair, Crowd

In a city this passionate about art, you're never far from a masterpiece to contemplate or debate.

FLYING SOLO

Get lost in history

Stadsarchief, the Amsterdam city archives, has exhibitions packed with paintings and photos. Come alone and let yourself really dig in. What's more, entry is free.

IN A PAIR

Ponder the contemporary

Impress your bestie by taking them to see the avant-garde art by emerging artists at Galerie Fons Welters in the Jordaan. Then head to one of the neighbourhood's arty cafés to dissect.

FOR A CROWD

Late-night musings

Want a Friday night out with a difference? Grab your friends and make for the Van Gogh Museum. The art and storytelling are always crowd pleasers, but during Friday lates you can enjoy live music and pop-up bars too.

MOCO MUSEUM

Map 3; Honthorststraat 20, Museumplein, Oud-Zuid;
///gave.breezy.snap; www.mocomuseum.com

Works by Banksy may get people through the doors here, but it's the cutting-edge exhibitions that makes them stay. Everything on display has a questioning take on society, whether it's an immersive look into the future of technology or a set of portraits that confront privilege.

STREET ART MUSEUM

Map 6; Immanuel Kanthof 1, Slotermeer, Nieuw-West;
///soft.blanked.shift; www.streetartmuseumamsterdam.com

Trust Amsterdam to turn the streets themselves into a museum. On this walking tour of the Nieuw-West neighbourhood, knowledgeable guides reveal the stories of immigration and environmental justice behind huge murals and tiny sculptures. It's mighty eye-opening.

COBRA MUSEUM OF MODERN ART

Map 6; Sandbergplein 1, Amstelveen;
///lighter.goods.evoked; www.cobra-museum.nl

Back in 1948, Amsterdam put the A in COBRA – a revolutionary art movement where artists from this city, Copenhagen and Brussels overturned tradition, painting abstract works inspired by children's drawings. COBRA may have ended in 1951, but this museum keeps that alternative spirit alive and inspires the city's avant-garde artists.

>> Don't leave without visiting the café for a cup of tea – well, you'll need somewhere to reflect on the bold paintings you've just seen.

Performing Arts

Theatre, cabaret, opera, ballet, music – you name it,
Amsterdam's theatres are always putting on a show.
Many performances are in English or with surtitles
so don't worry if your Dutch isn't quite up to scratch.

MUZIEKTHEATER

Map 4; Amstel 3, Plantagebuurt;
///mincing.wings.devotion; www.operaballet.nl

Half city hall and half home to the National Opera and Ballet, this 80s-built circular edifice was nicknamed "Stopera" – a protest slogan "Stop the Opera" against the demolition of other buildings to make way for it. The name has stuck, though it's since found a warm place in locals' hearts. Contemporary Dutch opera, boundary-pushing modern ballet, old classics – you'll find them all here.

ROYAL CONCERTGEBOUW

Map 3; Concertgebouwplein 10, Museumplein, Oud-Zuid;
///ranged.snails.pads; www.concertgebouw.nl

Classical music lovers know there's no beating the Royal Concertgebouw, widely admired for having some of the best acoustics in the world. It's the home of the Dutch Royal Orchestra, but there's the occasional rock, jazz or pop act here too. Friends treating themselves to a special night out book seats to enjoy the music of illustrious composers and performers like Mahler, Strauss and Cecilia Bartoli in the majestic hall. Our tip: look out for the free 30-minute lunchtime concerts, usually on Wednesdays (secure your ticket online).

ROYAL THEATRE CARRÉ

Map 4; Amstel 115–125, Plantagebuurt;
///inhales.clearly.fluid; www.carre.nl

This 19th-century monument is the crown jewel of the city's theatre scene. Depending on the night, the stage could be hosting live music or theatre, a comedy show or poetry recital. It's one of the best spots to catch musical theatre and something even dearer to local hearts: Dutch cabaret, witty songs and stories about the state of the world.

» Don't leave without admiring the elaborate 17th-century Amstel Locks over a drink on the theatre's riverside terrace café.

Shh!

Those living in Nieuw-West rave about De Meervaart (*www.meervaart.nl*), a contemporary theatre hidden away on the western edge of the capital. Why? It hosts a huge variety of progressive productions that represent the range of local experiences in the city. It also runs dance, theatre and DJ workshops for kids and young people living in Amsterdam. Community is front and centre here.

FRASCATI

Map 1; Nes 63, De Wallen;
///prep.improve.track; www.frascatitheater.nl

It's all about experimental theatre and dance at Frascati. Staging local and international companies, productions tend to be low on budget but high on inventiveness, which means you can see something unlike anything you've seen before without shelling out. Like, what if Macbeth ruled modern-day Brazil? That's the question at the centre of *The Walking Forest*. Or, who are we as human beings in a post-pandemic world? You'll find out in *Antibodies*.

DE BRAKKE GROND

Map 1; Nes 45, De Wallen; ///solution.issued.thigh; www.brakkegrond.nl

At the bottom of Nes (Amsterdam's theatre street) is this Flemish cultural centre. With cosy in-the-round seating, this is where locals come for cutting-edge theatre, dance and music (often mixed together) staged by their Belgian neighbours. Afterwards, they'll round off their evening with a meal at the venue's restaurant.

INTERNATIONAAL THEATER AMSTERDAM

Map 3; Leidseplein 26, Leidseplein;
///fairly.landed.ejects; www.ita.nl

If this Leidseplein monument looks important, that's because it is. It's the spot for "serious" theatre. Performances have included the likes of *The Things That Pass*, about life in the old Dutch East Indies, and

If you're after surtitles, sit in row 9 or higher so you can easily see them and the stage at the same time.

the biblical play *Judas*. Locals pour over these thought-provoking performances for hours on end, discussing possible interpretations in the theatre's café.

QUEEN'S ENGLISH THEATRE COMPANY

Map 3; Cullinanplein 1, De Pijp;
///jumbled.remodels.throats; www.qetc.nl

Tired of surtitles? This English-language theatre company in the CC Amstel Theatre is here to the rescue (English is the city's second language, after all). Anyone up for some Oscar Wilde, Alan Bennett or an adaptation of an early Hitchcock thriller? These are just some of the kinds of productions on show here.

PODIUM MOZAÏEK

Map 2; Bos en Lommerweg 191, Bos en Lommer;
///javelin.soccer.scouts; www.podiummozaiek.nl

Every day there's something different at this giant mosque-like theatre. Celebrating Amsterdam's diversity and multiculturalism, Podium Mozaïek is a community space for performers who represent the city's many cultures. You might come across anything from traditional Syrian dancing to Moroccan storytelling collectives to Caribbean music. And there's art exhibitions and drama workshops to top it all off, too.

» Don't leave without trying the oyster mushroom bitterballen at the theatre's café.

On Screen

Amsterdam's cinephiles are lucky to have some of Europe's quirkiest and most atmospheric film houses in their city. Whether it's arthouse or mainstream films you're after, there's a movie sanctuary for you.

FILMTHEATER KRITERION

Map 4; Roeterstraat 170, Plantagebuurt;
///restriction.jazz.defeated; www.kriterion.nl

Kriterion puts the shabby in shabby chic, but this cinema is part of the soul of Amsterdam. It's famous for its regular film festivals but you'll find all the current top indie films and even a blockbuster or two here the rest of the time. Discounted tickets draw a loyal student crowd who come to indulge their love of film at a bargain price.

Try it!
LEARN FILMMAKING

Every autumn, Kriterion, the EYE or LAB111 host the Imagine Film Festival. It's not just a chance to see top sci-fi, fantasy and horror films before their release – you can also take masterclasses from renowned filmmakers.

EYE FILMMUSEUM

Map 5; IJpromenade 1, Overhoeks;
///couch.teacher.weaned; www.eyefilm.nl

Squatting white frog, alien outcropping, giant futuristic sculpture –
this cinematic institution has lovingly been called loads of names
by Amsterdammers. And it's not just a museum – the EYE has
four screens mainly showing Dutch new releases and international
cult and classic movies from its massive archive. What with the
installations, special exhibitions and workshops too, this place is
always a huge hit with movie buffs, whatever they call it.

» Don't leave without hanging around the bar to take in the
gob-smacking views of the IJ River (pronounced like "eye", get it?)
from the wraparound terrace.

LAB111

Map 3; Arie Biemondstraat 111, Oud-West;
///fizzle.chuckle.flying; www.lab111.nl

A favourite of those in the west of the city, this three-screen theatre
shows hand-picked indie films, cult movies and old classics. And
anyone who works in the film industry has been to a premiere or two
here. Most locals don't consider their movie night complete without
pizza at the LAB111's laid-back Bar Strangelove (named after
Stanley Kubrick's classic film). And if you're wondering why there
are medical operating theatre-style lights in the bar, that's because
this big brick building used to be an anatomical pathology labor-
atory. That's not the only quirky feature – look up at the roof and
you'll see beehives.

FC HYENA

Map 5; Aambeeldstraat 24, Nieuwendammerham;
///cigar.wiring.typhoon; www.fchyena.nl

Indie cinema meets wine bar meets café with killer water views
at FC Hyena. The popular hangout has two screens that show
a curated mix of documentaries, kids' movies and recent Oscar
nominees (or likely future ones). But if you're here to chill out on
the brightly coloured sofas and enjoy a natural wine or cider
in the minimalist café, that's definitely cool too.

THE MOVIES

Map 2; Haarlemmerdijk 159–163, Haarlemmerbuurt;
///solving.ladder.pets; www.themovies.nl

Most beloved cinema in Amsterdam? Many would say that's
The Movies. This cosy picture-house is certainly the oldest still
in use, dating back to 1912. Friends head here in the evenings
to watch indie flicks and old and new alternative films in the
psychedelic Art Deco screening rooms. Join the locals and
round off your movie night with comfort food in the restaurant.

PATHÉ ARENA

Map 6; Johan Cruijff Boulevard 600, ArenAPoort, Zuidoost;
///pillows.obeyed.downward; www.pathe.nl/bioscoop/arena

This is the biggest, loudest cinema in the city. For those weekends
when Dolby Surround Sound isn't enough, families head to this
Pathé Arena mega-venue, which offers plenty of that and more,

Have a pre-movie drink at Brouwerij Kleiburg abbey, whose monks keep to the beer-making ways of yore. plus a serving of IMAX. Everything's bigger here: the glass staircases to the screening rooms, the cathedral-high silver screens and the booming sound speakers.

HET KETELHUIS

Map 2; Pazzanistraat 4, Westerpark;
///fizzle.chuckle.flying; www.ketelhuis.nl

Fancy seeing a truly local film? For the best selection, head to Het Ketelhuis, home of Dutch cinema. This movie theatre shows niche features, short films and documentaries, as well as some European films (they have English subtitles on Wednesdays).

PATHÉ TUSCHINSKI

Map 3; Reguliersbreestraat 26–34, Grachtengordel;
///sitting.edge.silly; www.pathe.nl/bioscoop/tuschinski

Jewish Polish immigrant Abraham Tuschinski built this opulent Art Deco movie palace in the early 1920s. An Amsterdam institution that tops countless "most beautiful" cinema lists, it hosts big premieres and all manner of blockbuster and arthouse offerings. The screen you should go for? The Grote Zaal (Great Hall) is the largest stage and stays true to its original elaborate glory, with plush armchairs and two-seater couches. Every film lover in the city has made a pilgrimage to this glorious shrine to the movies.

» **Don't leave without** getting the inside scoop on the histories and hidden corners of this landmark building with an audio tour.

Offbeat Collections

In the spirit of its creative, free-thinking nature, Amsterdam has many quirky cultural haunts, from fun micro museums to larger, often-overlooked collections.

ARTIS MICROPIA

Map 4; Plantage Kerklaan 38-40, Plantagebuurt;
///unusually.harsh.dart; www.micropia.nl

Microbes, microbes and more microbes: welcome to the world's first (you guessed it) microbe museum. Hosting an array of interactive exhibits, including body scans, a working lab and a multitude of microscopes, this modern museum turns the spotlight on these powerful little organisms. It's about time we got to know what we're made of.

THE HASH, MARIJUANA AND HEMP MUSEUM

Map 1; Oudezijds Achterburgwal 148, De Wallen;
///crop.surreal.heavy; www.hashmuseum.com

In a city that's world-renowned for its coffeeshops and cannabis, it's little wonder there are two museums dedicated to marijuana. This older one may be partially eclipsed by its nearby competitor, but the

Ask the staff all your cannabis questions and where to find the best coffeeshops (cannabis cafés).

exhibits really cover it all: culture, medicine, recreation. It's the perfect place to swot up if you're thinking of trying marijuana for the first time *(p10)*.

ELECTRIC LADYLAND

Map 2; Tweede Leliedwarsstraat 5, Jordaan;
///braced.howler.tracking; www.electric-lady-land.com

Anyone who's ever been to Electric Ladyland – the world's first museum of fluorescent art – can promise you that you will never have so much fun staring at rocks. These are not just any rocks, mind, but glowing, naturally fluorescent ones. If you can prise yourself away, enter the room of interactive black-light art next but, be warned, it will leave you feeling seriously off-kilter.

KATTENKABINET

Map 3; Herengracht 497, Grachtengordel;
///enjoy.hairpin.nipping; www.kattenkabinet.nl

Noticed how Amsterdammers never stop talking about cats? Their obsession is celebrated by this museum, packed with cat-related art in every form, including prints from headliners like Rembrandt and Picasso. Founder Bob Meijer set up Kattenkabinet in memory of his beloved ginger tom cat John Pierpont Morgan, who died in 1983 at the age of 17. The upper-class restraint of the 17th-century canal house contrasted with the unabashed feline fanaticism makes the whole thing a surreal trip down the rabbit hole – er, through the cat flap.

EMBASSY OF THE FREE MIND

Map 2; Keizersgracht 123, Grachtengordel;
///liquids.splash.promise; www.embassyofthefreemind.com

There are two kinds of people who are really into this library and exhibition space. The first are simply lovers of beautiful old books and prints. The others are fans of *Charmed* and other supernatural TV shows, who get to live out their fantasy, leafing through archaic books of astrology and alchemy that look like they might contain magic. Whichever camp you sit in, you're bound to be put in a trance by this shrine to all things mystical.

MUSEUM HET SCHIP

Map 2; Oostzaanstraat 45, Spaarndammerbuurt;
///learning.released.massive; www.hetschip.nl

When someone says this 1919 housing complex is Amsterdam School, they're referring to its uncannily curved style of brick

Amsterdam sometimes displays its treasures in the most unexpected places. Head to the Inntel Hotels Amsterdam Centre *(www.inntelhotels amsterdamzaandam.nl)* to sneak a peek at a mini-archaeology collection stowed in a cabinet across from the bar. The finds here have led archaeologists to believe that a castle might have stood on this site in the middle of the city in the 12th century.

architecture. At Het Schip you'll discover the social, political and artistic goals of this 20th-century art and architecture movement that aimed to give the working classes a better life by providing them with beautiful, quality homes. Getting up close and personal with the design details is just as fascinating as walking around the frozen-in-time post office and fully furnished apartments.

ALLARD PIERSON MUSEUM

Map 1; Oude Turfmarkt 127–129, De Wallen;
///lend.parting.developer; www.allardpierson.nl

Few local museum lovers make it to this cavernous museum of statuary, mummies and pottery before they've exhausted at least half the sites covered by their Museum Card membership. But that's no bad thing as there's almost never a crowd, which means the lucky few have this museum of curiosities all to themselves.

MUSEUM VAN DE GEEST

Map 4; H'ART, Amstel 51, Plantagebuurt;
///linen.level.pebble; www.museumvandegeest.nl

Want to see art that's raw and provocative? The Museum of the Mind (located in H'ART Museum) is all about Outsider Art: the self-expression of neurodivergent people, prison inmates and anyone outside conventional thought and society. Whatever you find here is sure to challenge you.

» Don't leave without browsing through the rest of H'ART, which displays art collections from all around the world.

Sip a beer at
IJ-KANTINE

Thirsty? Relax with a drink and waterside view on the sprawling terrace of this industrial-building-turned-restaurant. Back when huge cargo and warships were built at NDSM, workers came to this former "canteen" to have their lunch.

2

See some street art at
STRAAT MUSEUM

Marvel at the 150 pieces of massive street art on display at the STRAAT Museum. Based in a former warehouse, today it's both a national monument and the biggest outdoor canvas for graffiti in Amsterdam.

1

Docked on the NDSM pier, **Het Veronica** *was once the site of a pirate radio station. Today it hosts performances and art installations.*

NDSM-STRAAT

TT. VASUMWEG

MS. VAN RIEMSDIJKWEG

MS. VAN RIEMSDIJKWEG

NDSM

NDSM-PLEIN

NDSM-PLEIN

4

Finish up at
NDSM FUSE

End the afternoon by perusing the contemporary artworks on display year-round at the NDSM Shipyard. The exhibition changes every three months to reflect a different theme.

TT-NEVERITAWEG

3

Get creative at
PLLEK

Join an art workshop at this restaurant and cultural complex made out of old ship containers. Pllek also hosts art exhibitions, events and festivals.

Het IJ

0 metres   100

0 yards   100

An arty afternoon in
NDSM-Werf

Sat on the edge of the IJ, Nederlandsche Dok en Scheepsbouw Maatschappij (NDSM to its friends) was a busy shipyard for more than a century. Industry ceased in the 1980s and the space was left derelict – but not for long. Squatters and artists claimed warehouses once busy with shipbuilding and repairs, transforming the space into an edgy arts community. Today, NDSM remains a hub of creative activity; take an amble around to find the best of its artsy scene.

*Europe's biggest flea market, **IJ-Hallen**, takes place here once a month, with pre-loved clothes and antiques up for grabs.*

1. STRAAT Museum
1 NDSM-Plein, NDSM-Werf; www.straatmuseum.com
///crest.ruby.bless

2. IJ-Kantine
NDSM-Kade 5, NDSM-Werf; www.ijkantine.nl
///unroll.empty.affair

3. Pllek
TT Neveritaweg 59, NDSM-Werf; www.pllek.nl
///launched.jeep.massing

4. NDSM Fuse
NDSM-Plein 29, NDSM-Werf; www.ndsm-fuse.eu
///ledge.revisit.nurses

Het Veronica
///takes.revives.emphasis

IJ-Hallen
///jaunts.brush.pitchers

KLAPROZENWEG

ASUMWEG

rnelis Douweskanaal

Zijkanaal

NIGHTLIFE

Whatever day of the week, Amsterdam turns the volume up after dark: musicians take to stages, friends compete at games cafés and revellers dance until dawn.

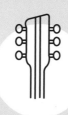

Cool Clubs

Looking for a proper night out? Amsterdam's got you. This is a city that's known 24-hour electronic dance parties since the 80s. Expect electric venues, top-tier DJs and a very late night (or early morning).

RADION

Map 6; Louwesweg 1, Nieuw-West;
///bonnet.toasted.spinning; www.radion.amsterdam

Housed in an industrial warehouse in an unassuming part of Nieuw-West, RADION is the ultimate rave spot. On a crowded dance floor, sweaty bodies move to pulsating techno beats, everyone making it their mission to party non-stop, which is easy enough given that this club has a 24-hour licence.

SHELTER

Map 5; Overhoeksplein 3, Overhoeks;
///among.milk.workouts; www.shelteramsterdam.nl

It doesn't get more underground than this club — literally, the inconspicuous entrance is through a hatch. Housed in the basement of the A'dam Tower, Shelter more than lives up to its name as a refuge for those hoping to let loose. With a booming sound system

 Been turned away at the door? Check out Vondelbunker in Vondelpark for another top night underground. | and a no-frills interior (think grey concrete walls and dark lighting), the club's focus is solely on finding transcendence through house and techno music.

RADIO RADIO

Map 2; Pazzanistraat 3, Westerpark;
///tuned.mixers.narrate; www.radioradio.radio

Who doesn't love a spontaneous night out? Radio Radio makes the perfect place for a last-minute dance club dash, thanks to its super casual dress code (hello trainers). Add great DJs and awesome music and we guarantee you and your squad will be dancing well until the early hours.

>> Don't leave without trying the oven-baked pizza at PizzaPizza, housed inside RadioRadio. Perfect sustenance to keep you going.

PANAMA

Map 4; Oosterlijke Handelskade 4, Oosterlijk Havengebied;
///engine.dawn.rooting; www.panama.nl

If international superstar DJs are your thing, head to Panama in the Eastern Docklands. Filling a vast electricity power station by the IJ River, it's one of Amsterdam's longest-running clubs. You'll find yourself dancing alongside a thousand other ravers to an electic programme of house, techno, hip-hop or jungle on any given night. Check out what's on to find the beat you connect with best and then let the music be your guide.

OT301

Map 3; Overtoom 301, Vondelbuurt; ///reds.train.coached; www.ot301.nl

Back in the 90s, this building was a squat where young creatives would come to, well, create. Now a legit non-profit, OT301 hasn't lost its free-spirited, artistic edge. Carefree locals gravitate towards this multi-purpose venue, taking a life drawing workshop in the day before dancing with abandon to dubstep and drum 'n' bass in the evening. It's not your usual club, but it works.

CLUB NYX

**Map 3; Reguliersdwarsstraat, Grachtengordel;
///rely.learning.manager; www.clubnyx.nl**

Every Amsterdammer's experienced an evening of revelry at this LGBTQ+ hotspot; Nyx was the Greek goddess of the night and the daughter of Chaos, so it all seems to track. The fun-loving crowds of regulars party all night long to Dutch hip-hop and pop anthems, making newfound friends on several dance floors as they go. There's even a DJ spinning tunes in the colourful bathroom, so the party never has to stop.

CANVAS

**Map 4; Wibautstraat 150, Weesperzijde;
///tinned.gamer.thanks; www.volkshotel.nl/en/canvas**

On the top floor of Volkshotel, this trendy venue starts the night as a chilled-out restaurant, but as the weekend hour gets late, the tables are cleared away and the space morphs into an alternative club. It's the domain of fashionable young professionals, who wash down *bitterballen* bites with G&Ts before moving to the dance floor, drinks in hand. If you need a break from dancing to hip-hop and underground house sets, come up for air on the roof terrace and take in the panoramic views.

» Don't leave without asking about the regular Badplaats Sessions, where you can take a dip in a hot tub, listen to live music and sip a cocktail on the rooftop. Pure bliss.

LOFI

Map 6; Basisweg 63, Westpoort; ///join.recently.developer; www.lofi.amsterdam

Once a bus garage, now a nightclub, Lofi is a powerhouse on the city's party scene. With a vast interior area and colourful outdoor courtyard, there's plenty of room to dance – and trust us, you'll be dancing. DJs keep the electronic beats thumping early into the morning (some events last until 5am) and the lively crowd are more than happy to keep on grooving.

Try it!
SPIN DECKS

Feeling inspired by Amsterdam's talented DJs? Book a beginner's workshop at DJ School Amsterdam *(www.djschool amsterdam.nl)* and learn the basic steps to spinning and mixing tunes.

Live Music Bars

For those nights when clubbing isn't on the cards, Amsterdam's chilled music bars provide the perfect soundtrack to catching up over drinks. Most of them let you rock up and listen for free, too.

MALOE MELO

Map 2; Lijnbaansgracht 163, Jordaan;
///bliss.averts.dating; www.maloemelo.com

Despite its moniker the "home of the blues", this scruffy dive bar is an in-the-know kind of place, tucked away in à residential area. Every night of the week, musicians and music lovers greet each other like old friends, chatting about their love for good sounds. It's not all blues tunes, either; expect plenty of rock, ska and country, too.

MAXIM PIANOBAR

Map 3; Leidsekruisstraat 33, Leidseplein;
///sprint.weekend.battling; www.pianobar.online

Looking for a good singalong? Swing by this Amsterdam institution. Maxim Pianobar never fails to put on a show, with master pianists tickling the ivories like there's no tomorrow and locals belting out well-loved classics. You'll pay a small fee for the luxury of being part of this epic form of karaoke, but it's guaranteed to be the best €5 you spend all night.

>> Don't leave without asking the pianist to play your favourite song – requests are always welcome at Pianobar Maxim.

JAZZ CAFÉ ALTO

Map 3; Korte Leidsedwarsstraat 115, Leidseplein;
///outreach.hype.coached; www.jazz-cafe-alto.nl

Follow the fashionable through the door marked by a huge saxophone into this cosy bar. There's a dark and sexy mood in the discreet 1920s-style space, where photos of iconic musicians hang from the walls and vintage brass lamps are dimly lit. Rock up by 9pm on any given night to nab a sought-after table, order a whisky and await a big name or a local talent. Then chill to the tunes till the early hours.

MULLIGANS IRISH MUSIC BAR

Map 1; Amstel 100, De Wallen; ///depend.changes.corals;
www.mulligans.nl

You can't go wrong with an Irish Bar, and Mulligans is one of Amsterdam's favourites. This ever-friendly pub is perfect for a low-key night out: spot the city's Irish contingent (and locals partial to a dry stout) slugging good Guinness as they catch up with old friends. Traditional live music usually begins around 9pm, with performers squeezing onto the tiny stage just inches away from the audience.

Solo, Pair, Crowd

No matter if it's you and the music or you and your friends, Amsterdam has a venue for all.

FLYING SOLO
Jazz things up
Rocking up solo to Bourbon Street is no biggie: this Leidseplein bar welcomes music lovers one and all. Grab a drink and settle in among the well-versed locals for a classic evening of blues, soul and jazz.

IN A PAIR
Time for a duet
Zoku's jazz nights may be sporadic, but they're worth waiting for. Sipping cocktails while watching up-and-coming musicians groove on this rooftop bar in Plantagebuurt is date night at its best.

FOR A CROWD
Good music, good company
Jordaan's Café de Koe is always a safe bet for a mellow – but memorable – night out with your pals. Expect Dutch comfort food to tuck into, classic boards games to banter over and a soundtrack of live local music.

THE WATERHOLE

Map 3; Korte Leidsedwarsstraat 49, Leidseplein;
///shadow.majority.mascot; www.waterhole.nl

As any local will tell you, a night in this grungy institution is a rite of passage. Every square inch may be covered with rock posters and electric guitars, but looks are deceiving. Yes, you'll witness rockers jamming, but folk and funk artists also keep all manner of crowds moving.
>> Don't leave without heading to the Tap and Dine restaurant on the first floor, where you can pour your own beer from a tap at the table.

DE NIEUWE ANITA

Map 2; Frederik Hendrikstraat 111, Oud-West;
///soak.tried.fruity; www.denieuweanita.nl

A night at this pub feels like you're at a jam session with your mates. Ring the bell to get in and the living room vibes (retro wallpaper and chesterfield sofas) are instantly palpable. Intimate acoustic sessions play out here, but for anything more upbeat (like an experimental punk-jazz band, say), the party moves to the larger back room.

THE CAVE ROCK CLUB

Map 3; Prinsengracht 472, Leidseplein;;
///staging.salsa.booklet; www.thecaveamsterdam.nl

While some rockers head to The Waterhole, those after more hardcore hits slink off to The Cave (an apt name for this basement bar). Hidden down by a canal, this haven for heavy metal turns it up to 11 on the weekends, with live music keeping fans headbanging all night long.

Comedy Nights

We get it, Amsterdam doesn't seem like a comedy hotspot but there is in fact an incredible stand-up scene here that locals can't get enough of. Here are some of our favourite venues.

EASYLAUGHS

Map 4; Nieuwe Achtergracht 170, Plantagebuurt; ///fooling.perfect.tablet; www.easylaughs.nl

Looking for a fun start to the weekend? Friday night is show night for improv troupe EasyLaughs, with two or three different shows over the course of the evening (you can buy a very well-priced ticket to one or all). Everything's made up on the spot, so you're guaranteed something special each time.

BOOM CHICAGO

Map 2; Rozengracht 117, Jordaan; ///suppose.swung.puzzled; www.boomchicago.nl

Seth Meyers, Jordan Peele, Jason Sudekis and Amber Ruffin all have something in common: they got their start here, at this outpost of Chicago's famous Second City comedy troupe. Several decades on, Boom Chicago is still the biggest improv game in town. There's a new show for every season, each themed to poke fun at Americans, the Dutch and modern society all at the same time. And they definitely will pick on the crowd, so be careful where you sit. If you want to be near the stage, opt in for dinner.

» Don't leave without asking about the courses and workshops, where you can get your improv feet wet.

THE JAM SOCIETY

Map 1; Nieuwezijds Voorburgwal 282, Spui;
///galleries.fortunes.kickers; www.jamvarietyshow.com

The most Dutch way to do comedy is cabaret, a unique take on the state of the world through music or spoken dialogue, going strong ever since the early 1900s. The uproarious cabaret shows at The Jam Society are presided over by host Daniel Matias Ferrer (who gets goofy), the house band keeps it quirky with improv jazz and a parade of variety acts (think clowns, magicians, musical comedy) fills in all the gaps. The absurdity of it all keeps locals coming back again and again. (Note: the venue often changes, so check online ahead of your visit.)

Try it!
TEST YOUR STAND-UP

Are you an aspiring comedian? That Comedy Thing *(www.thatcomedything.com)* is an indie stand-up collective with an open mic platform. Contact Roxy and Alexander through the website if you'd like to have a go.

TOOMLER

Map 3; Breitnerstraat 2, Apollobuurt, Oud-Zuid;
///glades.nights.split; www.comedytrain.nl

Amsterdam's top dedicated comedy club draws Dutch names who haven't yet crossed over into stadium status (note: anything marked "international show" will be in English). Arrive for the pre-show dinner to bag a good table, then settle in for a night of wide-eyed glee and uproarious laughter in this intimate, low-lit space that squeezes comedian and crowd together.

COMEDY CAFÉ

Map 5; IJdok 89, Westerdok, Westelijke Eilanden;
///froze.conveys.ladders; www.comedycafe.nl

This lovely space hosts a flurry of funny events every week. Well-known stand-ups like Gina Yashere and Stephen K Amos sometimes rock up, English-language shows are a common

Not many have heard of Paleis van de Weemoed *(www. palais-van-de-weemoed.nl)*, so this intimate theatre remains a closely guarded secret among locals. The dinner shows mixing music with comedy are always a laugh, but there's also plenty of burlesque, drag and other exciting cabaret acts on the menu too. Try not to get so distracted by the show that your food goes cold: it deserves some of the limelight too.

occurrence and the Comedy Embassy troupe brings together a mix of well-known local acts and newcomers. Arrive early to gawk out the floor-to-ceiling windows overlooking the IJ River before they draw open the curtains for the show.

MEZRAB

Map 4; Veemkade 576, Oostelijk Havengebied;
///text.unravel.spend; www.mezrab.nl

You'll be treated as family at storytelling hub Mezrab. Iranian owner Sahand runs the show while his mama doles out rich Persian soup, and more family and friends pour drinks. There are regular stand-up comedy nights, plus music and more, but the storytelling nights are the real soul of Mezrab; some are funny, some heartbreaking, many both. The setting is intimate, with the stage shunned in favour of a closely knit circle of couches and chairs. Most evenings are run based on donations – do chip in, they never get enough.

» Don't leave without asking about the storytelling workshops run by professional performers Farnoosh Farnia and Yinske Silva.

DE KLEINE KOMEDIE

Map 3; Amstel 56–58, Grachtengordel;
///pilots.hillside.light; www.dekleinekomedie.nl

Listen to comedians solving today's most pressing problems at the oldest theatre in Amsterdam, which offers a stage for both new and established Dutch talent. If your Dutch isn't quite up to scratch, there are occasional comedy nights in English, too.

Concert Venues

Indie rock, mainstream pop, jazz, dance, funk, techno. Whatever music you're into, Amsterdam's got your back. Venues large and small host big-name stars and performers on the road to world fame.

BITTERZOET

Map 1; Spuistraat 2 HS, Spui; ///drums.news.proofs; www.bitterzoet.com

Students averse to the mainstream own the night at this tiny indie club, conveniently located down the street from one of the University of Amsterdam's main campuses. The snug main room means no matter where you are, you'll always be close to the stage. Better yet, the entrance fee is very wallet-friendly.

PARADISO

Map 3; Weteringschans 6, Leidseplein;
///burn.restless.traded; www.paradiso.nl

You'd be hard-pressed to find a music lover who doesn't go misty-eyed at the mere mention of Paradiso. Visiting this renowned venue is something of a religious experience — fitting, given it's housed in a former church. Despite its cavernous size, there's a divine sense of intimacy to it all. On the main floor, big names play small sets against vitrage-covered windows, mesmerizing music devotees who pack out every inch of the space. Upstairs, lesser-known bands grace the stage of a smaller hall, on their way to becoming the next international star. But whether it's iconic musicians (past acts have included the Rolling Stones, David Bowie and Lady Gaga) or rising artists, rest assured the show will be sold out, so book well ahead if you want those bragging rights.

BIMHUIS

Map 4; Piet Heinkade 3, Oostelijk Havengebied;
///divided.dine.indirect; www.bimhuis.nl

The Muziekgebouw concert hall isn't just for contemporary classical music, it's also home to intimate Bimhuis, Amsterdam's temple to jazz. Jazz royalty like Kenny Wheeler and Steve Solo have graced the stage here, but that doesn't mean up-and-coming experimental musicians aren't granted the spotlight too.

>> Don't leave without strolling on the terrace of the Muziekgebouw with a chilled glass of wine in hand to take in the waterfront views.

Try it!
JOIN A JAM SESSION

Want to make new musical friends in the city? Bring your instrument to one of Bimhuis's regular jazz-jam sessions. All ages and abilities are welcome and sessions are free.

AFAS LIVE

Map 6; Johan Cruijff Boulevard 590, Zuidoost;
///entire.enter.incline; www.afaslive.nl

Music venues don't get more epic than AFAS, where big-name acts perform for crowds of thousands. On any given night, the enormous space throngs with young friends letting loose and chanting off-key to the sounds of their favourite bands.

OCII

Map 6; Amstelveenseweg 134, Oud-Zuid;
///fighters.agents.wiser; www.occii.org

The unofficial home of Amsterdam's underground scene, volunteer-run OCII is one of the last truly alternative music venues in the city. It was previously a squat so it's only fitting that it's now home to subversive acts, who (along with the cheap beers) draw in Amsterdam's cool crowd. Experimental punk, new wave and weird pop are the order of the day.

TOLHUISTUIN

Map 5; Tolhuisweg 3, NDSM;
///ventures.cross.lookout; www.tolhuistuin.nl

Join the magical garden party at Tolhuistuin, a cultural space with an outdoor stage throughout the summer. Hosting a big range of music styles from chamber to techno, its Garden Sessions see local acts perform in front of an audience lounging on garden furniture under twinkling lights. And when it's not

For other open-air concert venues, check out Caprera, Amsterdamse Bos and Woodstock 69.

summer or the weather doesn't play along, there's an indoor hall where no one's ever far from the stage, giving an intimate feel.

ZIGGO DOME

Map 6; De Passage 100, Zuidoost;
///winners.switched.betrayed; www.ziggodome.nl

If you thought that AFAS Live was big, wait till you see Ziggo Dome, the city's largest indoor arena built to host live music events. Expect tight security, long queues and pricey tickets but, hey, it's all worth it for a chance to party along with your mates to the biggest-name bands and artists in the world.

MELKWEG

Map 3; Lijnbaansgracht 234A, Leidseplein;
///blurst.boot.tangible; www.melkweg.nl

In a former dairy, the magically named Milky Way is one of the city's most sacred venues, having been a key player in the 60s counterculture scene. And it continues to push boundaries with a roster of exciting new talent, interspersed with well-established names. This is one of Amsterdam's top spots for dancing yourself to an ecstatic frenzy, whether to live music or on a weekend party club night.

» Don't leave without checking out Melkweg's exhibition space and flexitarian café MILK (entrance on Marnixstraat).

Games Night

Millennials are getting married, having careers, buying flats – but that doesn't mean the fun should stop. Embrace your inner kid and challenge your friends to a board game, virtual reality adventure or sing-off.

TONTON CLUB WEST

Map 2; Polonceaukade 27, Westerpark;
///tracking.pouch.later; www.tontonclub.nl/west

Bursting with retro arcade games, this is where Amsterdam's west-side hipsters come for a bout of nostalgia. Evenings are spent busting moves to Dance Dance Revolution, going square-eyed on Mega Tetris or battling it out on Daytona Racing – all to the soundtrack of concentrated thumb and feet tapping. Whoever comes last buys the next round of beers.

MOOIE BOULES

Map 4; Zeeburgerpad 3, Zeeburg;
///whizzed.director.remedy; www.mooieboules.nl

Amsterdammers take their games of boules seriously so when the weather plays foul (we all know it often does), they're thankful for the indoor bowling ground at this bar. Live bands and party

 If you'd rather play a classic board game or round of cards, there's plenty of these too at Mooie Boules.

vibes draw cool kids and serious bowlers alike for fun, competitive tournaments. Who really needs a French village when you've got Mooie Boules?

2 KLAVEREN

Map 2; De Clercqstraat 136, Oud-West;
///founders.porch.snacks; www.2klaveren.nl

Remember playing countless games of Monopoly, Scrabble and Backgammon with your family during the school holidays? Why not recreate the memories at this board game café – this time with a cold beer or tasty coffee. Be warned that 2 Klaveren gets very busy, with groups of friends competing over games, so arrive early in the evening to bag a table.

DUKE OF TOKYO

Map 3; Reguliersdwarsstraat 37, Grachtengordel;
///camper.smile.gift; www.dukeoftokyo.com

Pass by any brown pub of an evening and you're likely to see a bunch of old-timers enjoying a good sing-a-long. No surprises then that this karaoke bar fuels this singing passion among younger Amsterdammers, who challenge their mates to a sing-off in the more modern, Japanese style. Join them belting out their favourite 90s tracks in the private booths, styled to look like Tokyo neighbourhoods.
» Don't leave without trying the Yadokai Highball or Yuzu Slushy Daiquiri signature cocktails – good for Dutch courage.

CAFÉ DE LAURIERBOOM

Map 2; Laurierstraat 76, Jordaan;
///playful.toffee.navy; 623 3015

Grandmasters and newbies – all chess fans are welcome at this old brown pub. Challenge your friend to a game among the rickety stools and tables, but mind that you might have to wait a bit for your beer. Why? The bartenders are likewise pouring over their game and planning their next moves in between serving guests.

CHECKPOINT CHARLIE

Map 2; Nassaukade 48, Staatsliedenbuurt;
///result.lifters.guarded; www.cafecheckpointcharlie.nl

This Berlin-themed bar is where students and other 20-somethings compete at board games, pinball and pool between the well-worn retro seating and walls of bookshelves. DJs play a mix of millennial favourites and live indie bands regularly take to the floor.

VRGH ARENA

Map 6; Gyroscoopweg 102, Westpoort;
///waxing.sage.koala; www.vrgh-arena.nl

Want to fight your way through a dense jungle, dodge gruesome zombies or hurtle around a racing track? This virtual reality (VR) gaming house will scan your whole body to digitally transport you and your friends into a whole new world. Seriously cool.

» Don't leave without trying the free non-VR games at VRGH Arena, like XXL Jenga, foosball and air hockey.

Liked by the locals

"Checkpoint Charlie feels like home from the moment that you walk in. The friendly bartenders actually remember your orders, and it's the perfect place to make friends with strangers over a game of pool."

KAREN TURNER, ENTREPRENEUR

Late-Night Bites

*Feeling peckish? Whether you've been hitting the
clubs, comedy circuit or coffeeshops, this city
has plenty of places open all hours to fend
off those hunger pangs.*

GRILLROOM SHOARMA MESUT

**Map 2; De Clercqstraat 59, Oud-West; ///take.mailbox.hydrant;
www.grillroomshoarmamesutamsterdam.nl**

No ordinary kebab shop, this modern Turkish-style kitchen cooks
up the healthiest meal you'll find after a night out. Near the major
clubs in Oud-West, it's a hot favourite among partying west-siders
who satisfy their shashlik (skewered and grilled meat and veg)
cravings into the late hours to the soft echoes of lute tunes.

CANNIBALE ROYALE

**Map 1; Handboogstraat 17A, Spui;
///deep.skater.food; www.cannibaleroyale.nl**

Cannibale Royale serves some of the best ribs and burgers in
the city, or so say its dedicated fans who pop by for a late-night
dinner (it's open until 1am at the weekend) after bar-hopping
in Spui. You'll emerge blinking into the brightly lit street after

discovering the tenderest rib roasts, the most mouthwatering bavette and flat iron steaks, and the juiciest burgers you've ever tasted (there's plenty of veggie options too).

» Don't leave without dropping a pin on your Google map – you're gonna want to come back tomorrow to try the best Belgian fries in the city at Vlaams Friteshuis Vleminckx around the corner.

BAR-BECUE CASTELL

Map 3; Lijnbaansgracht 252–4, Leidseplein;
///finds.changes.fooling; www.castellamsterdam.nl

Long before you step through this cosy restaurant's doors, you'll smell the scent of charcoal and sizzling meat wafting down the street. Inside, hungry night owls feast on grilled-to-perfection steaks, extending their night out over a good gossip. All the tables are shared, so you'll likely make new friends here.

PATA NEGRA

Map 3; Utrechtsestraat 124, Grachtengordel;
///duty.bristle.sporting; www.pata-negra.nl

Fancy bringing the spirit of Spain to your night out? With cured hams hanging from the ceiling and bright ceramic tiles on its walls, this tapas bar feels like it was plucked from a busy street in Madrid and plonked right in the heart of Amsterdam. Long platters of *gambas al ajillo* (garlic shrimps), crunchy calamari and serrano ham, washed down with sangria, draw local nighthawks who love to party well into the night.

BURGER BAR

Map 3; Eerste van der Helststraat 62B, De Pijp;
///prosper.smaller.sweated; www.burgerbar.nl

After a Saturday night out in de Pijp, students find there's no more satisfying (or wallet-friendly) place to fuel up than this cosy spot where they get to build their own customized burger. Endless meat or vegan toppings join with fresh sauces to create the burger of your dreams.

WOK TO WALK

Map 1; Damstraat 44, De Wallen;
///stunts.inclined.clasps; www.woktowalk.com

The long queues that snake out of this Wok to Walk on weekend nights are testament to its super fresh Asian dishes that have taken the world by storm. Amsterdammers are rightly proud of this flagship branch, where it all started. Dig into your noodles at a communal table, perfect for bantering with fellow late-night revellers, or head out with your small orange box and eat as you walk.

THE BUTCHER SOCIAL CLUB

Map 5; Overhoeksplein 1, Overhoeks;
///tides.winters.remind; www.the-butcher.com/socialclub

Inside the hip designer Sir Adam Hotel, The BUTCHER Social Club is where young party-goers satiate their hunger after a night of dancing at the A'dam Tower's Shelter or Madam clubs. Patrons indulge in the creatively named gourmet meat and veggie burgers

and pose with classy cocktails on the terrace while watching
the sunset over the IJ River. It isn't just about the food though, The
BUTCHER is a true after-party hangout, with regular live DJs
and an old-school games hall.

>> **Don't leave without** trying out the pool, ping-pong and foosball
gaming tables, or the pinball machines.

NEW YORK PIZZA

Map 3; Leidsestraat 104, Leidseplein;
///feasts.escapes.pool; www.newyorkpizza.nl

This takeaway New York-style pizza joint is so beloved that
Amsterdammers are always prepared to join the long queues
to get their hands on a slice. While you wait, make up your mind
which of the juicy toppings you want to cover the thin, crispy base,
then grab your slice (even a New Yorker would be wowed by its
size) and follow the locals to perch on the fountain in Leidseplein
square. It's basically a rite of passage.

KAUFFMANN

Map 2; Reinier Claezsenstraat 4B, Oud-West;
///doctors.tenders.heavy; www.barkauffmann.nl

Tucked between blocks of flats in a residential street, this late-night
kitchen does only one thing but boy, does it do it well: crispy falafel
pittas with hundreds of different toppings. It's one of the top falafel
spots amid a boom in Middle Eastern restaurants that have sprung
up in the city. What more do you need after a night on the town?

A night out in
Indische Buurt

You won't find any cobblestoned, tourist-filled streets here. This historically industrial, working-class neighbourhood has had new life breathed into it, with old buildings transformed into bars and dining venues. Yes, it's still a bit rough around the edges, but it's creative — an old school gym has been converted into a club, a bathhouse is now a restaurant-bar and a water pumping station has a restaurant above it. The result? A buzzing hipster hub perfect for an evening out.

1. Bar Botanique
Eerste Van Swindenstraat 581, Indische Buurt;
www.barbotanique.nl
///surface.doormat.trooper

2. Bar Basquiat
Javastraat 88–90, Indische Buurt;
www.barbasquiat.nl
///cascade.rooting.gravy

3. Pompstation
Zeeburgerdijk 52, Indische Buurt;
www.pompstation.nu
///lies.grades.laptops

4. Studio-K
Timorplein 62, Indische Buurt; www.studio-k.nu
///puppets.collects.wage

5. Pizza'dam Oost
Sumatrastraat 68A, Indische Buurt;
www.pizzadam.nl
///boots.stamp.snapper

Dappermarkt
///grabbed.flanked.surround

Badhuis Oedipus
///devours.leaves.stumpy

Lozingskanaal

ZEEBURGERDIJK

**Sip cocktails at
BAR BOTANIQUE**
Begin your evening at this jungle-themed bar, housed in a former school gym.

EERSTE VAN SWINDENSTRAAT

DAPPER-PLEIN

DAPPER-BUURT

*Running since 1910, the **Dappermarkt** sells food from all over the world, reflecting the many nationalities who live in this neighbourhood.*

Enjoy live music at
POMPSTATION

Just show up – there's always live jazz playing at Pompstation bar-restaurant. Since 1912, this industrial building has been used as a pumping station and you can still hear the water being pumped out of the city.

Lozingskanaal

ZEEBURGERDIJK

3

ZEEBURGERDIJK

BORNEOSTRAAT

TIMOR-PLEIN

Dance at
STUDIO-K

Boogie the night away at a club night at Studio-K, a former school that doubles as a restaurant, cinema and concert venue too.

4

INDISCHE BUURT

CELEBESSTRAAT

SUMATRASTRAAT

JAVA-PLEIN

JAVASTRAAT

Chill at
BAR BASQUIAT

This edgy bar, styled after the late US graffiti artist Jean-Michel Basquiat, is a great stop for Surinamese street food.

2

Badhuis Oedipus *is a bar-restaurant converted from an old bathhouse. Its outdoor terrace is always packed on balmy nights.*

Grab a bite at
PIZZA'DAM OOST

If you're feeling peckish after your night of partying, fill up at this branch of the beloved Amsterdam-born pizza chain.

5

INSULINDEWEG

OOST

MOLUKKENSTRAAT

CELEBESSTRAAT

| 0 metres | | 200 |
| 0 yards | | 200 |

OUTDOORS

Amsterdam may be small, but it isn't lacking on the outdoors front. Come rain or shine, locals head out for a walk in the park, a leisurely bike ride or a swim in a lake.

Green Spaces

Did you know Amsterdam ranks as one of Europe's greenest cities? Locals are very proud of this fact, and rightly so. After all, there are countless parks sitting right on their doorstep.

AMSTELPARK

Map 6; entrance via Arent Janszoon Ernststraat, Buitenveldert; ///droplet.trunks.rooks; www.amstelpark.info

Welcome to Amsterdam's most whimsical park, created for the 1972 Floriade Flower Festival. Not a lot has changed since then: the gardens are still perfectly manicured and the 17th-century windmill still stands. That said, there's almost always something going on here, whether that's an outdoor concert, a food festival or art exhibition in the Glass House or Orangerie.

VONDELPARK

Map 3; entrance via Stadhouderskade, Vondelparkbuurt; ///stone.jolly.archives; www.hetvondelpark.net

In the swinging 60s, Vondelpark was the hangout of weed-smoking hippies, and it's retained that laid-back, anything-goes feel. Yes, it's the city's most popular park and the crowds can get pretty intense on a

If you're here in summer, check out the free weekend concerts at the park's Open Air Theatre. | sunny day, but it can't be beaten for people-watching. Join the throngs chilling amid scenic ponds, grassy fields and arty sculptures (see if you can spot the Picasso).

WESTERPARK

Map 2; entrance via Haarlemerweg, Westerpark;
///roaring.weekend.birds; www.westergas.nl

Think of Westerpark as Vondelpark's even cooler, younger sibling. A 19th-century gas factory has been converted into a community space, bursting with cafés, bars and event venues. And from this, the park's centrepiece, some of the city's lushest greenery spills out. Spread a blanket along the eastern lake, or sneak into the tall marshland grasses to find a quiet spot to meditate. It's always worth keeping an eye on the events calendar for some of the city's best food and music festivals.

FLEVOPARK

Map 6; entrance via Flevoweg, Indische Buurt;
///detection.upper.grower; www.flevopark.nl

Locals walk their dogs along the wild paths, runners jog around the large lake and, come the weekend, families feast on barbecues in this vast park. Bigger and wilder than many other green spaces in Amsterdam, Flevopark is also where birdwatchers flock to spot all sorts of water fowl among the idyllic marshy lake scenery.

» Don't leave without stopping for a drink and snack on the large waterside terrace of 't Nieuwe Diep Distillery inside the park.

OOSTERPARK

Map 4; entrance via Linnaeusstraat,
Oud-Oost; ///marathon.planet.placed

The locals of residential Oosterparkbuurt really rely on this much needed splash of greenery. They jog the maze of paths, meet for picnics in the meadows and practise outdoor tai chi on Saturday mornings. And there's always a crowd at Speaker's Stone at 1pm on Sundays – Amsterdammers love to speak their mind, after all.

REMBRANDTPARK

Map 6; entrance via Orteliuskade, Nieuw-West;
///stunner.estate.jungle; www.rembrandtpark.org

Game of football in mind? Organizing a frisbee tournament? Rembrandtpark on the western edge of the Canal Ring is the place for you. It's large and pretty quiet, so you and your pals will feel like you've got the place to yourselves. After all that running

Shh!

Looking for a little bit of R&R? Tucked away in Plantagebuurt, between the Portuguese Synagogue and the botanical garden, the tiny waterside Wertheimpark is often overlooked, even by locals.

Head straight for the grassy knoll along the canal, beyond the statuesque fountain – this spot never seems to draw a crowd. It's the perfect shady oasis in the city centre to sit and watch the boats go by. And breathe.

around, head to the park's southern end, where you'll find the Fashionhotel, home to the Floor17 roof terrace. Here you can refuel with a snack and take in the gorgeous views of the park and beyond. In summer, Floor17 also hosts movie screenings – the perfect end to a day in the great outdoors.

NOORDERPARK

Map 5; entrance via Nieuwe Leeuwarderweg, Volewijck; ///congratulations.splits.freezing; www.noorderpark.nl

This leafy lung of Amsterdam Noord used to be all green, no scene. Slowly but surely, though, more and more fitness facilities are opening up, luring health-conscious Amsterdammers – even from south of the IJ River. At any given moment, at least half of the park's visitors are here to break a sweat: at the outdoor gym or pool, in the Snakerun skatepark or at a workout bootcamp.

» Don't leave without rewarding yourself with a post-workout treat from Pompet, a gorgeous little café in the park.

ERASMUSPARK

Map 2; entrance via Mercatorstraat, Bos en Lommer; ///migrants.library.blast

In the west of the city, this little gem of a park feels like your own private island, thanks to the canals that bound it. It's got its fair share of grassy lawns for strolls and picnics, but it's the stunning flower garden, designed by local artist Elspeth Diederix, that draws locals for its resplendent year-round blooms.

On Two Wheels

Here, the bike rules. And it's not just for getting around, it's a way of life. From the lycra-clad to leisurely cruisers, everyone hits the hundreds of bike paths that weave through the city and beyond.

HAARLEM TO LISSE

Map 6; start at Haarlem train station; ///yoga.blaring.blues

This one is blooming lovely – quite literally. And it's seen as a pilgrimage by many locals who cycle the 35-km (21-mile) round-trip ride from Haarlem to Lisse in flower season (from April to May). The path leads through the dappled woodlands and daffodil fields of Heemstede and Hillegom into Lisse, the agricultural heartland of the Netherlands. The best bit? All the kaleidoscopic tulip fields, of course.

AMSTERDAM CENTRAAL TO DURGERDAM

Map 5; start at Amsterdam Centraal Station, IJzijde exit on Stationsplein; ///sunshine.crispy.raves

Head north from the city centre on a leisurely 18-km (11-mile) cycle and you'll find some of the cutest fishing villages in the country. Starting at Buiksloterweg, the trail winds through cobblestoned

Nieuwendam before reaching the fishing village of Durgerdam just northeast of Amsterdam. Here you'll hit up row upon row of pastures, criss-crossed by canals. End the day like the locals do, and head to the highest part of the Durgerdam dyke for a picnic with a view before cycling slowly back into town.

» **Don't leave without** stopping for a slice of apple pie on Café 't Sluisje's sunny terrace – it's enroute to Durgerdam.

AMSTEL RONDE HOEPROUTE
Map 6; start at Berlagebrug; ///vibes.translate.whom

Old windmills, grazing cows, thatched farmhouses. Sounds like picture-postcard Dutch countryside? That's exactly what you'll find along this 39-km (24-mile) circular route through polders. The path follows the Amstel River in the south of the city before leaving town and crossing grassy marshlands (birdwatchers, you're in for a real treat here) and the pretty village of Ouderkerk aan de Amstel. Stop for a lazy picnic in the grassland before looping around and heading back north into the city.

Try it!
CYCLE LIKE A LOCAL

Nervous about jumping on a bike? The lovely instructors at Koala Bike Lessons (*www.koalabikelessons.com*) will show you how to navigate rush-hour traffic and explain all the rules of the road.

VONDELPARK TO AMSTERDAMSEBOS

Map 3; start at Vondelpark; ///pelted.released.hang

Come rain or shine, Amsterdammers love cycling this path of a weekend. Starting at Vondelpark, the path threads through the Oud-Zuid borough before emerging on the shores of Nieuw Meer lake on the edge of Amsterdamse Bos. And it doesn't always end there: if they're feeling particularly energetic, there's another 14-km (9-mile) marked trail that starts and finishes at De Boswinkel visitor centre, taking them through the most spectacular parts of the forest.

ZAANDAM TO ZAANSE SCHANS

Map 6; start at Zaandam train station; ///lunch.knocking.fuel

With its old windmills and wooden barns, the village of Zaanse Schans is stunning, and locals find there's no better way to explore it than by bike. Follow the lead of Amsterdam's families by jumping on the train from Centraal station to Zaandam. From here it's an easy 5-km (3-mile) ride through a rambling expanse of tousled meadows, past willowy ponds to Zaanse Schans. Enjoy a backdrop of windmills, canals and dykes as you loop around the village.

WESTERPARK TO NIEUWE MEER

Map 2; start at Westerpark; ///tuxedos.hillside.removal

Convoy with friends swapping stories and catching up on their week as they ride out from Westerpark, stopping off at Sloterplas Lake for a dip (in summer) or just for the views. Highlights en route include super-cute Sloten village and Nieuwe Meer lake (where, if you're lucky, you'll spot shaggy highland cows). And the best spot to stop for a picnic? It's got to be the orchard at Tuinen van West nature reserve, where you can also pick your own fruit at the organic farm. Don't want the adventure to end? Turn the excursion into a weekend trip and stay the night at Freelodge in Tuinen van West.

RINGVAART TWISKE

Map 6; start at Twiskemolen; ///uses.jukebox.sour; www.twiskehaven.nl
After more of a picturesque pedal than a serious city cycle? We hear you. This 15-km (9-mile) path, which circles Het Twiske nature reserve, is the one for you. You'll pass through marshland and weave through picturesque ponds and lakes, with nothing but stunning nature views as far as the eye can see. Our kind of cycle.
» Don't leave without an evening drink and snack at Paviljoen Twiske as the sun sets over the lake.

AMSTERDAM CENTRAAL TO HAARLEM

Map 5; start at Stationsplein; ///sunshine.crispy.raves
Haarlem may be just a 20-minute rail journey from Amsterdam but, let's be honest, where's the fun in taking the train? A bike path connects Amsterdam Centraal with the beloved medieval city of Haarlem, offering loads of stop-in-your-tracks scenery along the way. You'll start by cycling northwest through Amsterdam's Sloterdijk neighbourhood and on to Halfweg before wending through Haarlemmerliede village and into Haarlem. Have a mooch around and grab a bite at a café on one of the cobblestoned streets — you've earned it.

Swimming Spots

As far as Amsterdammers are concerned, anything above 20°C is summer. With flip-flops and swimming gear at the ready, locals rush to take a plunge in open-water spots and outdoor pools.

BREDIUSBAD

**Map 2; Spaarndammerdijk 306,
Spaarndammerbuurt; ///points.deflect.bike**

With a large paddling section and water slides to boot, it's no surprise that this outdoor pool quickly fills up with families during the day. If you want to avoid accidentally winding up part of a kids' birthday party, join the early morning crowd when it's all about serious swimmers doing laps before work. Fair warning: they say the water is heated, but early birders don't always believe it.

STRAND DIEMERPARK

**Map 6; Diemerpark, IJburg; ///scary.wins.holiday;
www.amsterdam.nl/toerisme-vrije-tijd/parken/diemerpark**

Locals in need of a little solitude head to this gem of a lake in the quiet Diemerpark. Yes, the lake floor is a bit slimy, and yes, ducks and other birds bob about on the surface, but this is one of the best natural swimming spots in the city. After your swim, lounge on the long sandy beach, perfect for taking in the wide open-water views and the hustle-and-bustle of the busier parts of IJburg that you've left behind.

» Don't leave without taking in the perfect sunset views over the flat expanse of still water.

ZANDVOORT BEACH

Map 6; Zandvoort aan Zee, Zandvoort, Noord-Holland;
///sunbeam.indigo.munches; www.visitzandvoort.com

When the summer sun shines at the weekend, the masses start congregating on Centraal Station's puny, unprepossessing Platform 1 with coolers and beach blankets in hand. They're here to hop the 20-minute train ride to Zandvoort, the nearest North Sea beach to Amsterdam, with a vast stretch of sandy shoreline and bracing seawater for swimming. SUP-ing, rafting and surfing are big here too.

Shh!

Don't fancy a swim so much as a relaxing sauna? Head to the tiny Sauna Deco *(www. saunadeco.nl)* on Herengracht and feel all that tension slip away. Adorned with stained-glass windows and ornate furnishings, this gorgeous spa hosts two Finnish sauna cabins, a Turkish steam bath and a cold plunge pool. Beware, it's strictly birthday suits only, no bathing suits. Time to *really* get to know the locals.

GAASPERPLAS STRAND

Map 6; Gaasperplas, Nellestein, Zuidoost; ///clerics.retrain.takeover

For bucolic beauty that makes you feel like you've left the city without actually having to do so, the beach at the artificial Gaasper Lake nature reserve is what you need. Locals head straight to the southern mini-lake; cut off from the main body of water, it makes for a perfect tranquil swimming spot.

SLOTERPLAS STRAND

Map 6; Sloterplas, Slotermeer, Nieuw-West;
///weaved.nearing.hometown

In warm months friends and families pitch up with chairs and umbrellas on this urban beach. The Sloterplas Lake's sandy shoreline and clear, clean water get pretty busy in hot weather so make sure you turn up early to grab your patch. Oh, and if you're in town on New Year's Day, this is the best spot to join the freezingly cold Nieuwjaarsduik (New Year's Dive).

BUITENZWEMBAD MARINETERREIN

Map 4; Marineterrein (near Pension Homeland), Oostelijke Eilanden;
///uproot.poster.camera; www.marineterrein.nl

Although the inner bay of this former naval base isn't yet an official swimming location (it still needs to pass a few more tests for clean water), hardy locals regularly take the plunge at their own risk. Swimming space aside, when the weather's warm, Amsterdammers of all stripes grab their SPF and their flashiest

If you do want to swim here, check out the website, which has a low-down on the water quality.

swimwear to lounge along the docks and quays with postcard-perfect harbour views. It's the hangout to see and be seen on summer weekends.

FLEVOPARKBAD

Map 6; Insulindeweg 1002, Zeeburg;
///spit.flake.sampled; www.flevoparkbad.com

Looking for a wet and wild day outside? This massive swimming complex on the northern edge of Flevopark ticks all the boxes – an Olympic-sized outdoor pool, a shallow pool of the same size (with slides), heated water, lots of land to picnic in shade or sun, and snack spots in case you didn't BYO. The city is always threatening to convert this pool to indoor swimming, so if you're a fan of the space as it is now, consider donating to the cause to help keep it going.

MIRANDABAD

Map 6; De Mirandalaan 9, Rijnbuurt;
///riches.cheek.propose; www.amsterdam.nl/demirandabad

Welcome to Swimming City. No other swimming place in Amsterdam has so much choice. Warm, sunny weather? Plunge down the epic waterslide into the outdoor pool. Cold or pouring with rain? Bob up and down in the indoor pool with its very own wave machine. New to swimming? Take a lesson. This place has you covered.

>> **Don't leave without** heading next door to the Amstel Boathouse for an alfresco meal on the veranda.

On the Water

Laced with canals and fronted by beaches, Amsterdam is a city intimately connected to the water – and locals make the most of it. Join them sailing, canoeing and paddleboarding as soon as the weekend hits.

BOATY

Map 3; Jozef Israëlskade, Nieuwe Pijp;
///tedious.noodle.distract; www.amsterdamrentaboat.com

All of Amsterdam hits the water when the weather warms up, so hire a boat as soon as you can so you don't miss out. There are various rentals, but Boaty is one of the best, offering easy-to-drive small solar-powered electric boats at one of the lowest prices in the city. Grab up to five of your mates (each boat seats six) and get gliding along the canals. No boating licence or previous experience needed.

REDERIJ PAPING

Map 2; start from Keizersgracht 179, Grachtengordel or a location of
your choice; ///wisdom.tidying.stores; www.blueingreen.amsterdam

Skipper Paap founded these cosy boat tours so that he could share his huge love of his city. With a knowledge of canals like no other, he'll show you around – just tell him what you're interested in and you can decide on the route together. Even long-time Amsterdammers discover hidden corners and tiny canals they didn't know existed. What's more, Paap offers dinner packages too, if you're feelin' fancy.

» Don't leave without taking advantage of Paap's encyclopedic knowledge. Point to any building and you'll hear an interesting story.

THOSE DAM BOAT GUYS

**Map 2; start from Keizersgracht 96, Grachtengordel;
///resides.hotdog.cable; www.thosedamboatguys.com**

The super-friendly Dam Boat Guys are all about the puns. Take a pew aboard their boat and lap up their irreverent stories about the city – you'll be roaring with laughter alongside your crewmates before you know it. Not satisfied at tickling your funny bone, the boys have also collaborated with Mokums Mout to create two custom craft brews to tickle your taste buds as well. Cheers to that.

REDERIJ LAMPEDUSA

**Map 4; start from Dijksgracht 6, Oostelijke Eilanden;
///warriors.splint.long; www.rederijlampedusa.nl**

Run by refugees from Egypt, Syria, Somalia and Eritrea, Rederij Lampedusa's boat tours are like no other. Aboard you'll hear the personal stories of displaced peoples, and see Amsterdam through the eyes of centuries of immigrants. The whole thing's brought all the more alive by the fact that the boats themselves are refurbished vessels that were previously used to smuggle people across the Mediterranean Sea.

Solo, Pair, Crowd

There are so many more ways to cruise the waters of Amsterdam – with new friends, just the two of you or with the whole gang.

FLYING SOLO

Make a new friend

Hang solo on one of Rederij Friendship's popular saloon boat tours, which launch from the Red Light District. You'll soon get chatting with your fellow passengers.

IN A PAIR

Pedalos for two

When you want to put your friendship to the test, there's a fleet of pedal boats in the city moat across the street from the Rijksmuseum. You won't get far, but the fun is in the effort.

FOR A CROWD

Floating dinner party

Join the party at the Supperclub Cruise boat that leaves from Centraal Station every dinner time. Lounge in the cushty white dining room or air out on the top deck between courses of food and live music.

WETLANDS SAFARI

Map 6; Pick-up from Noord metro station;
///scouting.polo.office; www.wetlandssafari.nl

This five-hour canoeing safari takes you through the reed-packed wetlands just north of Amsterdam. Float past old windmills and villages to the chirping of black-tailed godwits and end with a walk along the polders and a picnic on the islands. You'll feel a world away.

VUURTORENEILAND

Map 4; start from Lloyd Hotel Dock, Oostelijk Havengebied;
///jelly.librarian.trousers; www.vuurtoreneiland.nl

Looking for something extra special? Try this: a boat trip to the Vuurtoreneiland restaurant. The tiny island is famous for its old lighthouse, fortress and sole other building: the haute-cuisine restaurant. The party begins with appetizers during the one-hour boat ride from Oostelijk Havengebied. On the island, a healthy feast awaits in a glasshouse with sweeping views. Be sure to book well in advance.

STAND-UP PADDLEBOARDING

Map 6; Canal Sup Amsterdam, Crynssenstraat 16, Oud-West;
///floating.tiger.skill; www.canalsup.nl

Locals don't just use their bikes to get around. SUP-ers see their city from a new perspective, peeking through the open windows of old canal houses in summer, gliding by riverbanks of autumn foliage and zig-zagging through semi-frozen water in winter. Hire a board at Canal Sup Amsterdam and join in year-round.

Nearby Getaways

Of course Amsterdammers love their city, but sometimes a change of scene or gulp of fresh air is just the ticket. Luckily, the city has many tempting places right on its doorstep.

FORTEILAND PAMPUS

40 minutes by ferry from IJburg; www.pampus.nl

Many moons ago, Amsterdam was defended from enemy attack by a circle of 42 forts on 42 islands. Over the years these forts gradually fell to ruin – including the biggest, Fort Pampus on Forteiland. The largely underground fort-turned-museum has an impressive dining hall and dungeon, but locals come to the island mainly to wander around the vegetable garden, have a picnic on the beach and a dip in the IJmeer (swimming gear is a must).

DELFT

1 hour by train from Amsterdam Centraal Station; www.delft.com

Home of the iconic Delft Blue ceramics, birthplace of painter Vermeer and resting place of William of Orange – yes, you've probably heard of Delft. And Amsterdammers know and love it just as much too, piling into the city to wander its hugely picturesque medieval streets. When they're ready for a break, day-trippers flock to the Postkantoor café near the centre, which has a cosy indoors and a terrace for sunny days.

THE HAGUE

1 hour by train from Amsterdam Centraal Station; www.denhaag.com

Those looking for a slice of culture head to Den Haag for some of the Netherlands' best museums, like the Mauritshuis (home to Vermeer's *Girl with a Pearl Earring*), the MC Escher Museum of illusionistic drawings and the darkly fascinating Prison Gate Museum. By the way, Amsterdam may be the official capital of the Netherlands but The Hague is the true beating heart of the Dutch government, so look out for the 13th-century Binnenhof, where parliament gathers and makes laws to this day, just a little way along from the Mauritshuis.

» Don't leave without visiting the Scheveningen district, with a long sandy beach, popular with sun worshippers and surfers.

UTRECHT

20 minutes by train from Amsterdam Centraal Station;
www.discover-utrecht.com

When Amsterdam's fashionistas have exhausted the shops in their city, they head to the centre of Utrecht, which is crammed with cool boutiques, quirky Dutch-designed labels and big brand stores. Naturally, any shopping trip wouldn't be complete without lunch. Some of the best restaurants are on the Oudegracht canal – actually on the canal, with terraces you could dip a toe off of. It's your perfect fashion fix with canal-ringed charm.

ZUIDERZEEMUSEUM

1 hour, 20 minutes by train from Amsterdam Centraal Station;
www.zuiderzeemuseum.nl

Young families love this open-air museum, where historical buildings (think: windmills, cheese shops, hairdressers) have been brought together to create an olde-worlde village. Make a hemp rope, try on old Dutch clothing and head back in time to 17th-century maritime life along the Zuiderzee ("Southern Sea").

VOLENDAM

50 minutes by 110, 136 or 316 bus from Amsterdam
Centraal Station; www.vvvedamvolendam.nl

Amsterdammers head north to fishing village Volendam to satisfy their seafood cravings. Follow the day-trippers past old wooden buildings to one of the harbour restaurants for the catch of the day and some of the freshest seafood you can find in the Netherlands. And as it's baby bro to neighbouring cheese capital Edam, Volendam also has a cheese factory and shop to boot.

» Don't leave without taking the short ferry ride to Marken island and getting a cool photo of its white lighthouse among the black rocks.

HET NATIONALE PARK DE HOGE VELUWE

45 minutes by train from Amsterdam Amstel Station to Ede Wageningen, then 20 minutes by bus; www.hogeveluwe.nl

Yes, this enormous national park is a haven for hikers and bikers, but it's the Kröller-Müller Museum that we're here for. This truly awesome museum makes the most of its stunning setting, with an epic sculpture garden blending works by the likes of Rodin, Jean Arp and Henry Moore with the natural woody surroundings. Indoors, the huge array of Van Goghs joins other masterpieces by Monet, Mondrian and Picasso. The collections have Amsterdammers returning month after month.

Try it!
MEDITATE IN NATURE

Want to really connect with nature? Join a meditation class in the Nationale Park de Hoge Veluwe (*www.anaya.nl*). You'll experience the elements of air, water, earth and warmth in a new way.

Nieuwe Meer

The **Vietnam Meadow** *used to be the site of political demonstrations, most notably against the Vietnam War in the 1960s.*

Fuel up at
BOERDERIJ MEERZICHT
This farm restaurant dating back to 1857 serves great *poffertjes* (mini-pancakes) and meat stews. Tuck in with meadow views of deer, peacocks and goats.

1

KOENENKADE

Bosbaan

BOSBAANWEG

Stroll around
GROTE VIJVER
Follow the loop trail that circles this large pond for an easy hike in the forest and then take a refreshing dip (weather permitting).

DE DUIZENDMETERWEG

3

Grote Vijver

NIEUWEMEERDIJK

2

Take to the water with
KANOVERHUUR AMSTERDAMSE BOS
Hire a canoe or pedal boat from this company or join a guided tour to navigate the park's waterways.

NIEUWE MEERLAAN

Gemaalsloot

Amsterdamse Bos

Tussen de Vijvers

A9

Klei Vijv

0 metres 400
0 yards 400

An afternoon exploring
Amsterdamse Bos

Come the weekend, locals flock to this massive forested park on the city's outskirts for a burst of fresh air. Built in the 1930s for the people of Amsterdam and three times the size of NYC's Central Park, it's long been a beloved refuge for Amsterdammers from all corners of the city. With loads of paths for walking and cycling, streams and ponds for kayaking or swimming, and quiet meadows to chill with a picnic, there's so much to explore that you could easily spend a full day here.

1. Boerderij Meerzicht
Koenenkade 56, Amstelveen;
www.boerderijmeerzicht.nl
///admires.sober.aquatic

2. Kanoverhuur Amsterdamse Bos
Grote Speelweide 5,
Amsterdamse Bos;
www.kanoverhuur-adam.nl
///lucky.pleasing.tougher

3. Grote Vijver
Amsterdamse Bos
///debate.tribe.muddle

4. De Heuvel
Amsterdamse Bos
///kindest.changing.cough

Vietnam Meadow
///voucher.resides.spotted

4
**Climb up
DE HEUVEL**
End your day by walking to the top of this artifical hill for sweeping sunset views over the park.

Karnemelske Vaart

Heuveltocht

With a little research and preparation, this city will feel like a home away from home. Check out these websites to ensure a healthy, safe stay in Amsterdam.

Amsterdam
DIRECTORY

SAFE SPACES

Amsterdam is an inclusive and tolerant city, but should you ever feel uneasy (or simply crave community), there's a host of spaces catering to different genders, sexualities, demographics and religions.

www.chabadamsterdamcenter.com
A cultural centre for Amsterdam's Jewish communities.

www.cocamsterdam.nl
An organization with advice and events listings for the LGBTQ+ community.

www.hostelle.com
A stylish and affordable female-only hostel in Amsterdam Zuidoost.

www.ibps.nl/home-2
A Buddhist temple for meditation and workshops.

www.maruf.eu
A source of information and meeting place for the LGBTQ+ Muslim community.

HEALTH

Emergency healthcare is covered by the European Health Insurance Card (EHIC) for EU residents and the Global Health Insurance Card (GHIC) for those from the UK. Non-emergency care is usually not free, so make sure you take out comprehensive insurance in advance. If you do need medical assistance, there are many pharmacies and hospitals across the city.

www.amsterdamcentralpharmacy.nl
A pharmacy in Centraal Station open every day, with a 24-hour vending machine next door for over-the-counter medicines. Doctor also on site.

www.amsterdamtouristdoctors.nl
Around-the-clock medical services with an online appointment-booking system.

www.dental365.nl
Emergency dental care with a 24-hour helpline.

www.ggd.amsterdam.nl
Amsterdam's public health service website, with links to a sexual assault centre and travel clinic.

www.hoteldoc.nl
Tourist doctors who will examine and treat you in your hotel at any time of day or night.

www.olvg.nl
Onze Lieve Vrouwe Gasthuis, a large hospital next to Oosterpark with 24-hour walk-in emergency services.

TRAVEL SAFETY ADVICE

Amsterdam is generally a safe city. Before you travel – and while you're here – always keep tabs on the latest regulations in Amsterdam and the Netherlands.

112
The telephone number to dial for all emergencies.

www.amsterdam.nl
Everything you might need to know about Amsterdam, from traffic alerts to construction projects.

www.politie.nl
The Dutch police portal: your first stop when something is stolen or for any other crimes.

ACCESSIBILITY

Amsterdam is an old city, but a socially conscious one, meaning that most (but not all) locations have been updated for better accessibility. These resources will help make your journey go smoothly.

www.ableamsterdam.com
The ultimate guide to Amsterdam for wheelchair users, covering restaurants, nightlife and general practicalities.

www.accessibletravelnl.com
A list of the most accessible hotels, attractions and activities in the Amsterdam area, plus mobility equipment rentals.

www.wheelchairtravel.org/ amsterdam
Links to information about accessibility and assistance at transport hubs like the airport and train stations.

INDEX

ACKNOWLEDGMENTS

Meet the illustrator

*Award-winning British illustrator David
Doran is based in a studio by the sea
in Falmouth, Cornwall. When not drawing
and designing, David tries to make the
most of the beautiful area in which he's
based; sea-swimming all year round,
running the coastal paths and generally
spending as much time outside as possible.*

With thanks

*DK Eyewitness would like to thank the
following people for their contribution to
the first edition of this book: Elysia Brenner,
Nellie Huang, Michal Mordechay, Rada
Radojicic, Tania Gomes and Casper Morris.*

THIS EDITION UPDATED BY

Contributor Roxanne Weijer
Senior Editor Lucy Richards
Senior Designer Vinita Venugopal
Project Editor Lucy Sara-Kelly
Indexer Helen Peters
Cartography Manager Suresh Kumar
Cartographer Ashif
Jacket Designer Laura O'Brien
Jacket Illustrator David Doran
Senior DTP Designer Tanveer Zaidi
Senior Production Editor Jason Little
Senior Production Controller Samantha Cross
Managing Editor Hollie Teague
Senior Managing Art Editor Priyanka Thakur
Art Director Maxine Pedliham
Publishing Director Georgina Dee

First edition 2022

Published in Great Britain by Dorling Kindersley Limited,
DK, One Embassy Gardens, 8 Viaduct Gardens,
London SW11 7BW.

The authorised representative in the EEA is
Dorling Kindersley Verlag GmbH. Arnulfstr. 124,
80636 Munich, Germany.

Published in the United States by DK Publishing,
1745 Broadway, 20th Floor, New York, NY 10019.

Copyright © 2022, 2024 Dorling Kindersley Limited
A Penguin Random House Company
24 25 26 27 10 9 8 7 6 5 4 3 2 1

A CIP catalog record for this book is available from the British Library.

A catalog record for this book is available from the Library of Congress.

ISSN: 1542 1554
ISBN: 978 0 2416 8016 2

Printed and bound in China.

www.dk.com

A NOTE FROM DK EYEWITNESS

The world is fast-changing and it's keeping us folk at
DK Eyewitness on our toes. We've worked hard to ensure
that this edition of Amsterdam Like a Local is up-to-date
and reflects today's favourite places but we know that
standards shift, venues close and new ones pop up in their
place. So, if you notice something has closed, we've got
something wrong or left something out, we want to hear
about it. Please drop us a line at travelguides@dk.com